Living Wisdom

Revised and Expanded

SECOND EDITION

David G. Benner, Ph.D.

WIPF & STOCK · Eugene, Oregon

Also by David G. Benner

Human Being and Becoming (2016)

Healing Emotional Wounds (2016)

Surrender to Love – Expanded Edition (2015)

The Gift of Being Yourself – Expanded Edition (2015)

Desiring God's Will – Expanded Edition (2015)

Presence and Encounter (2014)

Spirituality and the Awakening Self (2012)

Soulful Spirituality (2011)

Opening to God (2010)

Desiring God's Will (2005)

The Gift of Being Yourself (2004)

Spiritual Direction and the Care of Souls (with G Moon) (2004)

Surrender to Love (2003)

Strategic Pastoral Counseling, Second Edition (2003)

Sacred Companions (2002)

Baker Encyclopedia of Psychology and Counseling (with P Hill) (1999)

Free at Last (1998)

Care of Souls (1998)

Money Madness and Financial Freedom (1996)

Choosing the Gift of Forgiveness (with R Harvey) (1996)

Understanding and Facilitating Forgiveness (with R Harvey) (1996)

Strategic Pastoral Counseling (1992)

Christian Perspectives on Human Development, (with L Aden & J Ellens) (1992)

Counseling as a Spiritual Process (1991)

Counseling and the Human Predicament (with L Aden) (1989)

Psychology and Religion (1988)

Psychotherapy and the Spiritual Quest (1988)

Psychotherapy in Christian Perspective (1987)

Christian Counseling and Psychotherapy (1987)

Therapeutic Love (1985)

Baker Encyclopedia of Psychology (1985)

Wipf and Stock Publishers
199 W 8th Ave, Suite 3
Eugene, OR 97401

Living Wisdom
By Benner, David G.
Copyright©2018 by Benner, David G.
ISBN 13: 978-1-5326-9214-7
Publication date 5/20/2019
Previously published by Cascadia Publications, 2018

Dedicated To

All past, present and future members of
Cascadia – A Living Wisdom Community.

It has been my great privilege to learn
to access and live wisdom with you.

Contents

Preface   About This Book

The book you hold in your hands felt special to me from the beginning. Although authors should never be trusted to assess the significance of their own work, even when writing it I suspected this could be the most important book I have ever written. Many who have read the *First Edition* affirm this intuition.

My personal and professional focus for over 40 years has been understanding and facilitating human unfolding. Since wisdom is the capstone of both psychological and spiritual development it has been an implicit part of every book I have written. In this book it moves from the background to center stage and finally gets the attention it deserves – attention that, in my view, is crucial at this moment in human history.

Because wisdom cannot be reduced to words – either in the form of a definition or a set of principles for living – I have avoided both in what follows. My focus is not on understanding wisdom but on accessing, learning and living it. Like faith, wisdom is not real if it is not lived.

Wisdom flows from seeing through the new eyes of an awakened heart and expanded consciousness. The first astronauts who went into space to see the stars were most deeply impacted by seeing the earth from a new perspective. They came back changed people. The changes they experienced were the result of seeing through new eyes. In the same way, a new way of seeing lies at the heart of wisdom acquisition and living. And it lies at the heart of this book.

The understanding of wisdom that is implicit in what follows is grounded in the Christian sapiential (or wisdom) tradition. This tradition shapes how I see the world, others, and myself. I am unable, therefore, to say anything about wisdom that does not in some way reflect this tradition. Because I know this is also true of many of my readers I have included Scripture references and provided some of the background theological context for understanding wisdom.

This does not mean, however, that this book is either primarily for Christians or that others will find it irrelevant. The Christian wisdom tradition is not a set of beliefs to be embraced but a transformational path to be walked. This path does not simply lead to personal salvation but to wisdom that flows into compassionate care for the cosmos and all who inhabit it. This is a path that is available for those of any faith or none. It is a path that is available for all of us.

I am convinced that the spark that enters the world when even one person truly awakens and begins to live with wisdom and compassion is a light that the darkness and foolishness that surrounds us cannot overcome. I have written this book, therefore, with great hope.

May your engagement with what follows be much more for you than the mere reading of words. May it lead to a kindling of your heart, the illumination of your mind, and the transformation of your living. I am unable to imagine anything more important or exciting! I am so glad to have you share this journey with me!

David G. Benner

Part One   Understanding Wisdom

In Part One we approach wisdom as the precious jewel that it is – looking at it from multiple perspectives and reflecting on its many facets.
As we do so, our goal is more appreciation than analysis – each perspective on wisdom helping us to better understand its essential qualities and inestimable value.

"Wisdom is more precious than jewels,
Nothing else is so worthy of desire."
Proverbs 8:11[1]

1   Wisdom Knowing

I am delighted that you are holding this book in your hands. It suggests that, like me, you recognize the crucial importance of wisdom at this point in life – your own life and possibly, our life together on earth. Perhaps, also like me, you are not content to settle for mere knowledge but long to live with wisdom. If so, this book is definitely for you!

But, before you get further into it, let me offer a comment on the difference between wisdom and knowledge and a suggestion about how to best read this book as a way of learning to access wisdom rather than simply acquire information.

Wisdom and Knowledge

While knowledge comes from learning, wisdom comes from living. No one becomes wise merely by either the accumulation of information or the passage of time. However, while many people fail to become wise *as* they age, no one *actually* becomes wise *unless* they age.

Information leads to knowledge, but knowledge does not automatically translate into wisdom. Wisdom comes from living that is guided by seeing through eyes of an awakened heart and mind, and transformed consciousness.

In Buddhism this is called enlightenment. In Christianity it is usually described as acquiring the mind of Christ or Christ consciousness. Some refer to it as accessing cosmic consciousness. However, regardless of the language we use to describe it the important thing at this point to note is that it involves something much more profound than acquiring information. What it involves is a quantum shift in our inner world. It involves nothing less than a fundamentally new way of seeing and relating to everything in existence – to one's self, to others, to God and to the world.

> The Spirit of Wisdom inhabits all of creation and is our truest and deepest self.

My goal in writing this book, therefore, is *not* to pass on gems of wisdom. My goal is to help you learn how to access and live the wisdom that is grounded in the Spirit of Wisdom that inhabits all of creation and is our truest and deepest self. And my way of doing this will be to attempt to facilitate in you the awakening and transformation that allows wisdom to begin to flow from your depths.

But let me take you back to something I just said to be sure that you notice its importance. I said that the Spirit of Wisdom (my way of identifying God as the source of all wisdom) inhabits all of creation and is our truest and deepest self. This means that wisdom comes from living in alignment with the One I am calling, the Spirit of Wisdom. It also means that since the Spirit of Wisdom inhabits all of creation and is our deepest and truest self we are already deeply connected to what we seek. This is why accessing wisdom has less to do with acquiring knowledge than learning to see through new eyes and a new, higher level of consciousness – what I describe as Christ consciousness.

Wisdom knowing is not so much knowledge *about* wisdom as a way of knowing and living *with* wisdom – a way of knowing and living that involves not just the mind but also the heart.

The Wisdom Way of Reading this Book

The portal to wisdom is the awakening and transformation of our hearts and minds. Walking through this doorway does not lead us to a pool of knowledge but to a way of knowing. I would describe this way of knowing as wisdom knowing.

Most of what people claim to know is a product of their minds. You might say, for example, "I know I exist because I am capable of thought," (I think therefore I am). This "knowing" is clearly the fruit of the mind. Or you might say, "I know God exists because I believe the Bible." But once again, because beliefs are construals (formulations or understandings) they too are the fruit of mental processes.

Wisdom knowing is not dependent on the senses and can never be reduced to beliefs. It is deeper than either of these things. It is knowing that emerges from hearts and minds that are awakened, integrated (or we could say, aligned) and transformed.

I will have much more to say about this later. But leaving it here for the moment brings us to the matter of how to read this book in order to most fully access wisdom, not just gain knowledge of it.

The default mode of reading is reading with our minds. The mind excels in sorting and classifying information. What we sort and classify we then slip into the mental file folder that seems most relevant to that bit of information. But sadly, the information then tends to just stay there – in a library of knowledge that has little relevance to how we actually live.

However, much like trying to read a book of poetry searching for knowledge, reading this book exclusively with your mind will not serve you well. In fact, if you primarily read it this way you will likely be disappointed and will probably conclude that it contains very little worthy of being called wisdom. You might find things that are interesting but they shouldn't be confused with wisdom.

How we read either supports the default mental level of organization of consciousness or it helps us shift into our deepest centre – our heart – and thereby open ourselves to the possibilities of the awakening and transformation from which wisdom flows. This brings us to the alternate way of reading that can facilitate accessing wisdom.

What I would suggest is that you read what follows contemplatively and slowly. Read a little bit (perhaps no more than a paragraph or two) – then ponder it – then read it again – and then reflect on it further. Rather than reading to get something from the book I would suggest that you read it with the sort of openness that allows it to get you. But for this to happen, that openness will need to involve both your head and your heart.

While you read, pay as much attention to what arises within you as you do to the words you read. Notice what disturbs you; what excites you; what offers hints of hope or peace; what rings true in your depths. Don't be afraid to think about what you read but don't settle for only engaging with it through your thoughts.

I would also encourage you to resist the temptation to try to decide whether or not you agree with what you read. Sorting information in terms of agreement or disagreement is a good indication that you are reading with your mind because the mind specializes in making distinctions and judgements. Heartful reading is reading that is continuously

> The heart is oriented toward wisdom, beauty, harmony and wholeness.

interspersed with pondering. Don't judge or analyze whatever you notice arising within you. Just welcome and reflect on it. Hold it with openness and hospitality, and with an absence of judgment.

Pondering is a gentle way of engaging with things. It lacks the intense focus of the more familiar activity of thinking. When we ponder we turn things over in our mind – viewing them from different perspectives in order to understand the fullness of whatever we are reflecting on. This is what I call mental pondering.

Heart pondering is noticing what arises in our depths in response to something – feelings, memories, longings, hopes, and fears. This is what Mary the mother of Jesus did at the Annunciation when she pondered what she had heard from the angel in her heart.[2] Mental pondering adds enormous value to normal thinking but heart pondering broadens both the inner reflective space and the tools you bring to the pondering. Don't settle for mental pondering. Begin to also learn and practice heart pondering.

Reading in this way does not conflict with reading with the mind. But it definitely goes beyond it. Notice your questions but don't be distracted or preoccupied by them. Hold them gently rather than demanding an immediate answer to them. But while keeping one eye on the words you are reading keep the other on what arises within you in response to those words. That is the core of heartful reading.

The heart is naturally oriented toward wisdom – just as it is oriented toward beauty, harmony and wholeness. It will signal its recognition of these things with an inner sense of resonance. Something will ring true. Watch for that feeling of inner resonance. This is the way of wisdom knowing.

I realize that reading in this way may be unfamiliar. But, I strongly encourage you to try reading with your heart. It will help you cultivate and deepen new dimensions of learning, knowing and living wisdom.

Noticing and then responding to the invitations that come with this sense of inner resonance is also a very important part of wisdom knowing. I can't predict what you will feel invited to do but the important thing is that you trust your heart and respond with consent to the invitation, whatever it may be. If you are paying attention to your heart you will recognize these invitations. Responding to them is the route to the awakening of your heart, and seeing through the eyes of your awakened heart is the path to living wisdom.

As we proceed I will have much more to say about all of these things. But because I will not be simply presenting information but attempting to facilitate wisdom knowing, I will be speaking to both your heart and your mind, not just to your mind. This is why the journey we will be taking in this book will be more like walking a meandering, spiral path than following a straight line to a destination. We will touch on certain core issues repeatedly, each time from a slightly different perspective. Walking this path will allow things to be slowly woven together within you, something that is quite different from filling up mental file folders of information.

So, please be patient as I lead you along this wandering, circuitous route. Even if it appears unclear to your mind where we are headed at any point, your heart will understand.

So glad you have joined me on this journey! I am honored to be able to accompany you on it!

Pausing
to Ponder

At the end of each chapter I will offer you a chance to stop and reflect on what you have read. Since the wisdom tradition understands the heart as the fullness of the mind, the heart includes the mind. What I invite at these points, therefore, will include opportunities to ponder with both your head and your heart. Reflect on my words and then notice the things that have arisen within you in response to them.

Let me offer several things to get you started.

1. *If, as I suggested, the creative Spirit of Wisdom inhabits all of creation and is your truest and deepest self, this means that you already possess a deep and intimate connection to wisdom. How aligned do you feel yourself to be, at this moment, with this deep, personal source of all wisdom? How deeply aligned would you like to be? How willing are you to trust that you are already connected to the deep wisdom you seek?*

2. *What was hard about trying to pay attention to your heart, not merely my words and your thoughts, as you read this chapter? What most surprised you about reading this way?*

I encourage you to offer the same hospitality to whatever arose in you as you read this first chapter. Perhaps you want to review it again. If you do, note the things you want to ponder now or at some point before you proceed to the next chapter. And then make time to reflect further on these things.

Additional Readings and Things to Ponder

For more on the heart and its relationship to the mind see David G. Benner, *Human Being and Becoming* (Grand Rapids, MI: Brazos, 2016); also, Cynthia Bourgeault, *The Wisdom Way of Knowing* (San Francisco, CA: Jossey-Bass, 2003). Both these books offer a good discussion of the importance of the heart in accessing wisdom, and offer help in how to move your processing and knowing from the mind down into the heart.

2   Wisdom and its Foil

When I think of someone I would call wise the first person who comes to mind is my mother. She was a woman of few words who spoke only when she had something to say, never simply because she felt she had to say something. Her speech was sparse because she was comfortable with silence and comfortable within herself. But whenever she said something it was filled with warmth and gentleness and it usually reflected a larger perspective on the issue at hand.

I recall doing something very foolish at age 5. Undoubtedly it wasn't the first foolish thing I did and it certainly wasn't the last, but it comes to mind when I think now of my mother.

It was a bright, but very cold, mid-winter Canadian morning. Stepping out onto our front porch I was fascinated by the crystalline structures that had formed on our brass mailbox. They sparkled in the sunlight, as if they were trying to be freed from it to take flight. I drew closer to look at them carefully. Suddenly I felt an irresistible urge to taste them. I suspect you know where this story is going! My tongue immediately froze to the metal and, letting out a muffled yell, my mom quickly appeared at the door with a smile on her face – and, after a moment, some warm water. Still smiling, all she had to say was, "That was a foolish thing to do, but I suspect you already know that." With those few words she gave me a label for what I had done, and an opportunity to reflect on it. Thinking back on this it is now my turn to smile as I see in this encounter a key ingredient of learning to access wisdom – reflection on life experience. My mother was, therefore, my first wisdom teacher.

But my mother's focus on wisdom went far beyond such practical matters as not licking frozen metal or touching hot stoves. She had a slim, leather-bound copy of the Psalms and Proverbs from which she or my father read a short passage every morning at breakfast and another at dinner. Proverbs 3: 5-6 was her favorite passage and through repeated readings its words were etched on my young soul:

> *Trust in the LORD with all your heart,*
> *and do not lean on your own understanding.*
> *In all your ways acknowledge him,*
> *and he will direct your path.*[3]

And, in case there was any reason to worry that I or my brother might forget these words, they were also framed and on prominent display in our living room!

I wonder if you also have someone that comes quickly to mind when you think of wisdom. Or perhaps it is someone who you think of as singularly foolish.

Wisdom is often best seen in contrast to its foil – foolishness. The difference between the wise and foolish person is so obvious that the wisdom literature of the world makes extensive use of stories of fools to illustrate the distinctives of wisdom. Think of Jesus' story of the fool building his house on sand while the wise person builds on rock. The difference is easily recognized. Or think of his parable about one blind man leading someone who is also blind, and the danger they both face of falling into a pit. Foolishness is often best recognized by the absence of wisdom and wisdom by the absence of foolishness.

The Dalai Lama was once asked what most surprised him about humans. As the story goes, he answered that humans sacrifice their health in order to make money. Then they sacrifice money to recuperate their health. Then they are so anxious about their future that they do not enjoy or truly live in the present. Then they live as if they are never going to die, and die having never really lived.

> The wisest person often does incredibly foolish things and fools sometimes show moments of stunning wisdom.

Although the Dalai Lama never mentions wisdom, his description of foolishness clearly identifies at least part of what wisdom involves.

Wise Fools

But the danger of seeing wisdom and foolishness as opposites is that we easily tend to miss the fact that the wisest person will still often do incredibly foolish things and fools can, at times, show moments of stunning wisdom.

Even King Solomon (described in the Bible to be the wisest man on earth, wiser even than the collective wisdom of ancient Egypt[4]) displayed rather incredible lapses of wisdom. Honored throughout the ancient world for his wise judgment and vast knowledge he also did some incredibly foolish things. Ignoring God's warning about being careful to protect his heart, he married 700 women and had at least 300 concubines who, we are told, turned his heart from Yahweh.[5]

But we don't have to go back into ancient history to find examples of wise fools. Think of contemporary people in significant positions of leadership and influence who do really stupid things. It shouldn't be hard for you to quickly think of a number of religious leaders, politicians and other public figures who fit the bill. And perhaps you can also find examples in your family or circle of friends.

Much more helpfully, think of the incredibly stupid things you have done in your own life – things you have never wanted anyone to know about, things that even now you may have trouble acknowledging. Ouch! Now it's suddenly clear why we are so much more comfortable thinking of others as foolish and ourselves as – if not wise, at least generally displaying common sense. It is hard to admit that we also are sometimes incredibly foolish. But until we do, we fail to recognize that wisdom and foolishness are twins that live together in the human soul.

Crazy Wisdom

C. G. Jung described our inner fool as expressing a kind of crazy wisdom that, by challenging conventional wisdom, points us toward true wisdom. Looking back on his life at age 85 he said that since human nature is temperamentally set against wisdom he had often found it necessary to pay the price of being foolish in order to access true wisdom.[6] Just as we cannot recognize silence apart from having known noise, or light apart from knowing shadow, so too, it seems, wisdom is only recognizable in relation to foolishness.

Jesus offers us a classic, example of the apparent craziness of wisdom. Think of the seemingly foolish things he taught and lived:

- To find your life you must first lose it
- To achieve eternal treasures you must abandon all your earthly possessions
- The last will be first and the first will be last
- The meek and poor in spirit, not the powerful, will inherit the earth
- Laboring is the real rest
- Giving is the way to receive
- Becoming enslaved is the way to be truly free
- Yielding is the way to conquer, and
- Dying is the way to truly live

Is it any wonder the official religious wisdom figures had to kill him? Yet, seen through the eyes of faith and across the distance of time, clearly what Jesus was offering qualifies as hidden wisdom – seemingly crazy but profoundly true and wise.

Wisdom often needs to be cloaked. The court jester has always hid behind humor to deliver his message. And, as Jung noted, sometimes it may be necessary to pay the price of being (or at least appearing to be) foolish in order to access true wisdom. Most people are fools who think they are wise. And those who actually are wise will often appear to be fools.

For most of us, the path to true wisdom will not be as simple as it seemed to be for Solomon. God asked him what he most deeply desired, Solomon asked for wisdom, and God gave it to him.[7] For the rest of us, the route to wisdom is through life – through all its absurdity, foolishness, missteps and their consequences. And, despite what we want to believe, that path has no short-cuts.

Pausing to Ponder

1. Take a few moments to reflect on Jung's assertion that it is sometimes necessary to pay the price of being foolish in order to access true wisdom. Has this ever been true for you? What does this tell you about the relationship between wisdom and foolishness?

2. What have you learned from your own foolishness? If you seem to have learned nothing, consider that perhaps this is because you have not had the courage to name and own your own foolishness. Only that which has been welcomed and shown hospitality can be truly transcended.

3. Think of anyone you might have encountered who you might call crazy-wise. What deeper wisdom did their lives reflect? What

aspects of your understanding of reality did they challenge and what, in retrospect, might you have been able to better learn from them?

Additional Readings and Things to Ponder

Georg Feuerstein's, *Holy Madness: The Shock Tactics and Radical Teachings of Crazy-Wise Adepts, Holy Fools and Rascal Gurus* (New York: Penguins, 1992) offers an engaging discussion of fools for Christ, eccentric Zen masters and spiritual clowns who, throughout history have challenged people's common sense understandings of life and, by their apparent foolishness, pointed others toward deeper wisdom.

3   Doomsday Wisdom

You may not feel that we are on the brink of Doomsday but according to the keepers of the Doomsday Clock (members of the *Bulletin of the Atomic Scientists', Science and Security Board*), recent events have brought us terrifyingly closer to global annihilation. In early 2017 they advanced the Doomsday Clock to just two and a half minutes before the midnight of a very-high probability man-made global catastrophe, and in the opening days of 2018, moved it forward by another 30 seconds.[8] The only previous time when, in the estimation of this esteemed body of scientists, we were at this level of risk of global annihilation was in 1953 when the US tested the first hydrogen bomb and the clock was set at two minutes to midnight, this later being relaxed at the end of the cold war.

However, the nuclear threat is not the only cause for alarm. In November 2017 more than 15,000 scientists from 184 countries signed a "Warning to Humanity" that was published in the Oxford University Press journal, *Bioscience*. It focused on the global crisis we are facing related to freshwater availability, marine life depletion, ocean dead zones, forest loss, biodiversity destruction, climate change, and the implications these things have for the sustainability of life on earth.[9] Predictably, some have responded to this warning with charges of scaremongering. But prophets have always delivered unwelcome messages and we ignore their warnings at not just our own peril but in this case, the peril of the earth.

However, you don't need the opinion of scientists to sense that we are currently living in very troubled times. For many, the world just seems to be getting crazier every day. Consider, for example:

- The attack on the basic moral value of truthfulness by those in power who believe that saying something makes it true, then further eroding any meaningful concept of truth by talk of "alternate facts"
- The seemingly unstoppable and ever–increasing gap between the richest 1% of the world and the remaining 99%,
- The rapid decline of liberal democracies and rise of fundamentalist movements and authoritarian governments led by divisive strong-men thugs whose real concerns do not extend beyond the advancement of their personal interests
- The continuing presence of terrorism, mass murder and other forms of violence that, even when considered apart from formally declared wars, take the lives of more than 1.6 million people globally each year and leave millions more traumatized and deeply damaged.
- The rising tide of hatred, xenophobia, white supremacy movements, racism, and religious intolerance, or,
- The increasing polarization of societies into groups that hate and mistrust each other, crippling governments and depriving public life of even the façade of civility that has for decades characterized domestic and international relations.

A growing disorientation, shock and sense of doom pervade much of the West as we join the rest of the developing world in life on the edge of hopelessness and despair. Some fear that not only is civilization in a state of retreat, human consciousness itself seems to be in a period of rapid regress. How could this have happened so quickly? How are we to come to terms with a future that suddenly feels much darker and more precarious than many of us have known in our lifetimes?

Wisdom in an Age of Unreason

In the midst of this I often find myself talking with people about wisdom. Usually this emerges in the context of conversations about current events and when this begins to lurch toward despair I often find myself commenting on what I feel is the urgent need for wisdom. Sometimes this shifts our focus from the current affairs to the nature of wisdom and the question of how it can be cultivated. But at many other times, the possibilities of wisdom in an age of unreason seem too slim to withstand the onslaught of despair and hopelessness.

So, what is the path of wisdom in the face of the global problems facing us in the early days of the twenty-first century? And perhaps even more basically, what would wisdom look like in the face of these sorts of global challenges?

Many who talk with me about wisdom seem to understand it as something like common sense. To them, honesty and truthfulness need no justification, and upholding these values just seems like common sense. It also just seems like common sense to take seriously anything like a strong consensus of scientists or other specialists when they offer warnings or advice, and to take concrete steps to attempt to reduce poverty, address the conditions that fuel global terrorism and take better care of our planet.

> No problem can be solved from the same level of consciousness that created it.

But obviously, common sense doesn't get us past the instinctive way in which humans seek to protect self-interests and preserve the status quo. Nor can we assume that humans are wired to do the sensible thing. The evidence seems to suggest that our capacity for irrationality is at least as great as our capacity for rationality. And one person's common sense seems often to be another's total lack of sense.

Others who talk with me about the wisdom we need to deal with the global challenges we face don't assume a base of common sense. Often they believe that education is the answer – or, at the very least, that education can go a long way toward teaching shared values that can facilitate life together and a sustainable future. Values education strives to shape thinking and behavior in ways that prepare people for living together as responsible global citizens and many people are hopeful about the possibilities these sorts of programs have for the cultivation of wisdom.

But, as we have already noted, wisdom is not simply knowledge or even understanding. Many of the people who have been most responsible for getting us into the problems we currently face have been highly intelligent and knowledgeable. But they haven't been wise.

Wisdom is sometimes defined as the ability to use knowledge in ways that support the common good. Clearly, the world is better for all when it is best for everyone – including the marginalized, voiceless, and oppressed, and earth itself. But is education up to the task of overcoming self-interest? Can we really count on it to carry the freight of getting people past entrenched blind spots, self-delusions, rationalizations, and other expressions of egocentricity and fundamental dishonesty? Speaking personally, I do not think we can.

Awakening and Transformation

No problem can be solved from the same level of consciousness that created it. We cannot deal with present global realities by employing the tools that created them. We need to approach them with new minds and new hearts. We need to approach them with a new level of consciousness.

Wisdom comes through seeing and engaging life from a new, larger perspective. Education might, at its best, facilitate this but seldom does it go deep enough. Nothing less than a change of consciousness will help us deal with the realities we face as global neighbours in lifeboat earth.

I do not believe that the path through the troubling present realities that lead many to lose hope is a return to some perceived-to-be glorious past. That is simply the rhetoric of populist politicians. The only way through these developments that truly transcends them rather than simply reacts to them is the path of wisdom.

Nothing could be more important for the future of the world and for our own personal lives than humans learning to access and live the wisdom we desperately need to deal with the world's most pressing geo-political challenges. It is the hope for our world – and beyond it, for the cosmos.

Pausing

to Ponder

1. What do you see as the most important threats to the world at this moment in human history? How have you been responding to the direction you see things moving in terms of these issues?

2. What helps you avoid (or minimize) despair and continue to try to be part of the solution rather than part of the problem?

3. How would you define wisdom, and how might that understanding help us with the global problems you see as most important?

Additional Readings and Things to Ponder

I have said enough in this chapter about the darkness we presently face in our world. What I offer through additional readings are resources to help combat despair through active engagement with the global challenges we face. One person can make a difference. One small group can make an even larger one, and one community even more.

Sabrina Alkire & Edmund Newell's *What Can One Person Do? Faith to Heal a Broken World* (New York, NY: Church Publishing, 2005) offers concrete steps individuals and groups can take to make a lasting difference in the world. Their focus is the eight, highly achievable, Millennium Development Goals set by the United Nations in 2000.

In their book, *Active Hope: How to Face the Mess We Are In Without Going Crazy* (Novato, CA: New World Library, 2012) Joanna Macy and Chris Johnstone focus on how to maintain hope by seeing the global problems we face through new eyes and then, from this platform, engaging with them in ways that make a difference.

4   Natural Wisdom

Recently I was given the opportunity to spend three weeks on an expedition ship exploring the coastal regions of Antarctica and some of the Antarctic and Sub-Antarctic islands. Without question it was the most incredible three weeks I have ever spent anywhere, and nearly a month later I am still at a loss for words to describe the magnitude of the impact it had on me.

Of the many species of birds and mammals we saw on this trip, none was more amazing than the Wandering Albatross. With a wingspan of up to 11.5 feet (3.5 m), these giant birds spend years on the wing without ever once touching land or stopping to rest on the water – easily covering 800 miles a day (1,300 km) at sustained speeds of 50 miles an hour (80 km/h) or greater. Distances covered by them in flight are hard to measure but one was tracked and documented as travelling 4,000 miles (6,500 km) in twelve days, another with making a complete circumnavigation of earth in just 46 days. But perhaps most astoundingly, they do this without flapping their wings. Scientists describe how they do this as dynamic soaring – a form of flight that uses extremely little energy (less energy spent than they spend sitting on the ground) and involves flying into the wind in a way that allows them to soar at three times the speed of the wind.

This, however, is not the albatross's only astounding ability. They are also expert navigators and weather forecasters. In stable weather conditions they have been tracked making almost ruler-straight trips from distant foraging areas several thousand miles away, maintaining their course by means of an internal magnetic reckoning that fixes their position relative to the earth's magnetic field. Weather prediction is also crucial since dynamic soaring requires that the wind speed be higher than 18 mph (29 km/h). The only time they land on water is if they are becalmed, but because getting back in flight on the water consumes so much energy they rely on sophisticated barometric sensors to choose their direction up to 24 hours prior to the arrival of a change of weather, thereby following a course that offers the highest probability of sustained winds.

So at home are these birds in flight that they spend the first six of their years without ever touching land. And then they somehow find their way home to their breeding ground on the same rocky outcrop of the same island in the vastness of the Southern Ocean each time the breeding cycle calls them back home.

What can we say about these amazing birds? They are not likely very good at quantum physics, writing poems or abstract thinking but they do seem to be at one with what they were created to be and appear to tap into a deep source of wisdom that flows from that oneness. Or perhaps we can simply say that they appear to be aligned with the Spirit of Wisdom that inhabits all of creation and is the ground of everything that exists.

The Wisdom of Nature

But albatrosses are not unique in the deep sources of wisdom that they tap into. Wherever we turn in nature we see the same picture.

Consider the common ant. In spite of possessing the super-human ability to lift and carry 100 times its body weight it can be swept away by a single drop of water. However, the most astounding ability of these little creatures is not weightlifting but their capacity to form a coordinated super-organism that can accomplish things that no individual ant could ever accomplish. Acting together they have the ability, for example, to make a living bridge by clasping onto each other's limbs as they stretch across a chasm – adjusting the bridge shape moment-by-moment to maximize efficiency and strength.

> Nature reflects the wisdom of the Spirit of Wisdom because it remains aligned with its source.

Individual ants are like the neurons in our brain – each one being quite limited in what it can do but in combination, becoming a formidable force. Just imagine if humans were to regularly tap into the same wisdom and were willing to cooperate in the same way!

Or consider the wisdom of plants. While animals can choose their environments, plants must be able to adapt to constantly changing conditions without being able to move. Because of this, plants have evolved remarkably complex sensory systems – forms of sight, smell, taste, touch and memory – that allow them to be aware of their environment and its patterns of change, and then adapt.

Adaptation is a fundamental component of the wisdom of everything that has life. In plants, leaf size represents an adaptation to patterns of temperature fluctuation (smaller leaves coping better with larger fluctuations than larger leaves), the availability of water, and the need to capture an optimal amount of sunlight for conversion into the chemical energy that they require for life.

Leaf shape reflects a myriad of tiny adaptations over evolutionary time, each small adaptation then genetically passed on to future generations. An individual plant may then go even further to change its leaf characteristics to adapt to changes in its immediate environment. Under present conditions of dramatic climate change these adaptations may prove to be their salvation and ours. However, as we currently witness the extinction of many species of plants and animals each year we recognize the limits of adaptation, even in the realms of nature that seem to be most deeply attuned to the Spirit of Wisdom that inhabits all of creation.

Natural Alignment

Nature reflects the wisdom of the Spirit of Wisdom because nature remains fundamentally aligned with the source from which it flows and by which it is sustained. The alignment does not guarantee its survival. Scientists suggest that the cause of the extinction of dinosaurs was likely dramatic climate and geological changes that interrupted their food supply. But these same changes allowed ants to survive and thrive. So, survival of any one species is not guaranteed. However, tapping into the cosmic ground of wisdom does guarantee that things realize more of the fullness of being that is theirs by virtue of their very existence.

In all of creation, alignment with the Spirit of Wisdom that is the ground of our being is a challenge only for humans. Tulips, rocks, bacteria, wolves, trees, stars and ants all naturally tap into the ground of their being and the source that guides their existence. Only humans seem to lose touch with this state of alignment. Misalignment seems to be our default state. Theologians suggest that this is a result of sin. Using slightly different language, I would simply describe it as a consequence of alienation from the truth of ourselves and from the Spirit of Wisdom within whom we exist and have our being.

The Bible tells us that the whole of creation groans as it waits in pain for its liberation from the bondage of decay.[10] This suggests that the whole of creation, not just humans, may also lack full alignment with its source and may not yet experience its fullness of being. However, it seems to me that the non-human world is more closely aligned with our common source than humans, this being why wisdom is in such short supply amongst those of us who think of ourselves as the capstone of creation.

We have so much to learn from what St. Francis of Assisi described as Brothers Moon, Wind, Air and Fire; Sisters Sun and Stars; and Mother Earth.[11] But that learning will never meaningfully happen as long as we think of them as objects separate from us that exist for our pleasure and consumption. It will require that we first begin to see them as our brothers and sisters – or, in the language of the Lakota of North America, our relations.

Pausing

to Ponder

1. How do you understand the wisdom behind things like the immune system of the human body; migrating birds like the Wandering Albatross; or the fact that animals safely leave their habitats before tsunamis, volcano eruptions and hurricanes?

2. Edmund Burke – the Irish philosopher and political theorist – once said, "Never, no never, does nature say one thing and wisdom another." How do you understand what he is suggesting by this?

3. If it is true that nature reflects a fundamental and deep wisdom, how do you account for things like natural disasters that do not seem obviously favorable to humans? What do these events tell you about the nature of wisdom and our perspective on it?

Additional Readings and Things to Ponder

In *The Wisdom of Wilderness: Experiencing the Healing Power of Nature*, Gerald G. May describes the wilderness as our natural state and unpacks the implications of this natural state for human well-being. This book also provides a helpful discussion of the way in which outer events and experiences can facilitate inner transformation.

Whereas the power of Gerald May's writing is the power of an outstanding story teller, *The Nature of Wisdom: Inspirations from the Natural World* by Bruce W. Heinemann offers a more contemplative engagement with the subject. This is a book of photography that is interlaced with inspiring quotes, all focusing on the wisdom of the natural world.

Finally, let me recommend a book that, on the basis of its subtitle, you might judge to not be for you – *The One-Straw Revolution: An Introduction to Natural Farming* by Masanobu Fukuoka. Far from being primarily about agriculture, what this book offers is an opportunity to see the world through the eyes of someone who is convinced that nature always knows more than human beings. It is the fruit of the author's life-long effort to learn to comprehend nature's way of doing things. It certainly has implications for farming but it has equally important implications for cooking, eating and living. In essence, it is, as many reviewers have said, a book about the wisdom of nature.

5   Indigenous Wisdom

Wisdom flows from seeing the world through eyes that recognize the sacred interdependence of everything in existence. But rather than discuss this as an abstraction, let me illustrate what it means by looking at a group of people who live with this awareness at the center of their consciousness – the Indigenous Peoples of the world.

All My Relations

The Lakota people are part of the Sioux Nation that occupies much of the Great Plains of North America. They are a proud people with a rich heritage who live, like all Indigenous Peoples, with stable awareness of being deeply woven within the web of life.

Central to the Lakota understanding of what this means is the phrase, "Mitakuye Owas'in" – which, in English, translates as, "You are all my relatives." One of the most profound symbols in the Lakota culture is the circle which carries the same meaning – the belonging of all within the larger whole that embraces each individual, each family, each nation, and the whole world and all its inhabitants.

But it is their sense of what constitutes a family that most clearly communicates this sense of interconnectedness. A family in Lakota culture, like families in all Indigenous cultures, could never be restricted to parents and their biological children. If we are all related in the circle of life, family will always be much larger than what we non-Indigenous People think of as the nuclear family since it will always include what Lakota people refer to as "all my relations."

Lakota often speak this phrase in communal gatherings. What they are expressing is their gratitude for all those who form part of their family, this typically involving a group of 250 – 350 people that includes their:

- Biological brothers, sisters and all cousins
- Biological mother and all her sisters and female cousins
- Biological father and all his brothers and male cousins
- Maternal grandparents and grandparents of mother's cousins
- Paternal grandparents and grandparents of father's cousins
- All the grandchildren of these grandparents
- Your own biological children
- Your grandchildren and all the great grandchildren of all the grandparents and their cousins
- All the friends of the family who have been adopted by ceremony and carry the responsibilities of care for all members of this new family as well as their own, and
- All the relatives of your marital partner[12].

But this is still not the full extent to their family. Also included in any Lakota family are the non-human nations – the plants, animals, rocks, stars and everything else in creation. All these nations are considered equal and part, therefore of one's family.

Lakota may not have heard of St. Francis of Assisi but they share with him a deep sense of Brother Sun, Sister Moon and Mother Earth – as do all Indigenous Peoples of the earth.

Sometimes this understanding is turned into the Lakota prayer that gives the underlying knowing fuller expression:

To the Creator, for the ultimate gift of life, I thank you.

To the mineral nation that has built and maintained my bones and all foundations of life experience, I thank you.

To the plant nation that sustains my organs and body and gives me healing herbs for sickness, I thank you.

To the animal nation that feeds me from your own flesh and offers your loyal companionship in this walk of life, I thank you.

To the human nation that shares my path as a soul upon the sacred wheel of Earthly life, I thank you.

To the Spirit nation that guides me invisibly through the ups and downs of life and carries the torch of light through the Ages, I thank you.

To the Four Winds of Change and Growth, I thank you.

You are all my relations, my relatives, without whom I would not live. We are in the circle of life together, co-existing, co-dependent, co-creating our destiny. One is not more important than the other. Each evolves from the other and yet each is dependent upon the others. All of us are a part of the Great Mystery.

Thank you for this Life.[13]

This prayer is an expression of gratitude. But there is something equally important that goes along with this sense of gratitude in Indigenous cultures and that is a sense of responsibility. Knowing the interconnectedness of all things leads to knowing our responsibility for all of creation. Let me briefly describe how this works itself out in another Indigenous culture – this time, the Kogi living in the Sierra Nevada Mountains of Colombia in South America.

Helping Little Brother Remember

The Kogi are the only Indigenous civilization to have survived the Spanish conquests in South and Central America. They did this by fleeing the lowlands of coastal northern Colombia they had inhabited for at least six centuries before the conquistadors arrived and moving into the mountains where they have now lived for the past 500 years.

The Sierra Nevada arises from the sunny coasts of the Caribbean tropics to the chilly, snow-capped peaks that reach a height of 17,000 feet (5,200 m) above sea level. Adapting to life in the mountains was not easy for them. However, they had long considered the mountains to be sacred, calling them "Mother" and understanding them to be the heart of the world. So, when they found their new home within the sanctuary Mother provided, they also discovered with new depth their reason for existence.

The Kogi believe that it is their sacred calling to be the caretakers of the earth. This starts with caring for the mountain range they inhabit but it extends to the whole earth. And they take that responsibility very seriously. Their whole life is built around meditation and other sacred rituals designed to keep the earth in balance, as well as the more practical ways they have developed to live in harmony with their local mountain environment.

43

They refer to themselves as Older Brother and they call everyone else (except members of the few other Indigenous tribes in the region) Younger Brother. Although they lived in seclusion from modern civilization until very recently, they had long been keeping a keen eye on Younger Brother. They watched as he destroyed the coastal wetlands and shoreline, built hydroelectric

> Knowing the interconnectedness of all things leads to knowing our responsibility for all of creation.

dams, and began to mine the lower levels of the mountain and pollute the air. And they witnessed the resulting landslides, floods, deforestation, drying up of lakes and rivers, and the death of trees and other forms of vegetation.

Finally, in 1990 they decided that they had to initiate contact with Younger Brother since it was alarmingly clear that he was destroying the earth. He seemed to have forgotten that he was part of it. They felt that their isolation was no longer defensible as they needed to warn Younger Brother of the catastrophic future facing the planet if he didn't change his ways.

The event was documented in a celebrated BBC documentary, but their words went unheeded. Showing incredible lack of understanding of interdependence of biological systems, scientists disputed what they took to be the ridiculous Kogi argument that what happens in the coastal lowlands could affect life high in the mountains.

The Kogi could not understand how this could be. How could the scientists who studied the natural world as they did fail to know what they knew? How could Younger Brother not understand that the earth is a living body and if they damaged even a small part of it, they damaged the whole? And how could they not understand that if they damaged the body of the earth they also damaged themselves? And so they retreated and did what they could to repair the damage to the parts of the mountain that were their habitat. But they remained deeply concerned about what Younger Brother was doing to the earth and their obligation to help him remember what he had obviously forgotten.

Twenty-three years later they summoned the filmmaker who had made the first documentary back to their home to renew the message, now with an even increased sense of urgency. This time they took more control over the messaging by turning the project over to their spiritual leaders – the Kogi Mama.

The Mama of the Kogi community are the enlightened ones. They are raised in darkness for their formative years and then receive 18 years of training before being judged ready to carry their full spiritual responsibilities. The time in darkness is designed to help them learn to connect with the cosmic consciousness that they consider to be the source of the wisdom of the world. It is this gift that ultimately they want to give to Younger Brother. But first they felt that had to teach Younger Brother the delicate and critical interconnections that exist between everything within the natural world. They believe that only after this reality becomes a deep part of consciousness can Younger

Brother learn to tap into the cosmic consciousness that is available to all humans.

In the resulting film, *Aluna*[14], the Kogi Mama try to teach Younger Brother that what happens anywhere on earth affects the whole of earth. They present as their evidence of this, once white-capped peaks of their mountains that are now brown and bare, lakes that are parched and trees that are dying on their lands because Little Brother has forgotten that everything is interconnected.

The core of the film is their urgent appeal to Younger Brother to respond to the needs of the earth in order to keep the world in balance. Tuning into this cosmic wisdom is, they argue, the most important task of any human being. This time, a specialist in ecosystem restoration, a professor of zoology, and a world leader in marine biology back up the views of the Kogi. And this time the documentary gets the attention it deserves and becomes immensely popular around the world.

Sadly, however, the habitat of the Kogi continues to be destroyed. However, rather than responding with despair, the Kogi leaders have recently turned to tourism to get their message to the world. Even though they are doing this on a very small scale to limit the impact of visitors (who have to hike for 3 days through the jungle and up the mountain to get to them[15]) it is hard to realize how far this takes this small community that has existed for a thousand years in isolation beyond their comfort zone. But their keen sense of their calling as caretakers of the world drove them to take this drastic step.

Pausing
to Ponder

1. Think how your perspective on life, as well as your sense of self, would be different if you were to consider yourself deeply connected to all of life and to every human regardless of race, politics or religion.

2. Then push this further and consider what would change in your way of relating to the world if you took seriously the Christian understanding that everything in existence is held in Christ (Colossians 1: 15-17) – a place in which there is no Jew or Gentile, not even male or female. This is the Christian framework for understanding our deep interconnectedness to everything and everyone that exists. Ponder that framework and its implications.

Additional Readings and Things to Ponder

Richard Wagamese, *Embers: One Ojibway's Meditations* (Madeira, BC: Douglas & McIntyre, 2017). This is a book of gentle reflections on creation as the author draws inspiration and wisdom inspiration from life in the Pacific North-West bush. In many ways this book is an Indigenous counterpart to Brother Lawrence's classic, *Practicing the Presence of God* as Wagamese describes how daily life provides an opportunity to bring him closer to the Creator.

Robin Wall Kimmerer, *Braiding Sweetgrass: Indigenous Wisdom, Scientific Knowledge and the Teachings of Plants* (Minneapolis, MN: Milkweed Editions, 2015). In this book, the author, a botanist and professor of plant ecology, shares legends from her Potawatomi ancestors that illustrate contemporary scientific understandings of plants. A master story-teller, she brings the two lenses of scientific knowledge and Indigenous wisdom together to identify gifts and lessons that the natural world offers if we have eyes to see and ears to hear.

Finally, if you have not already seen it I encourage you to watch *Aluna*, the film about the Kogi. In many parts of the world if can be accessed on Netflix, in others it can be downloaded free of charge or for a nominal rental, and in yet others it can be purchased through Amazon. Details about its availability can be found at http://www.alunathemovie.com/

6   The Science of Interconnectedness

Hopefully you are beginning to understand that wisdom involves seeing from a larger perspective. This is why I have described wisdom as the fruit of the transformation of consciousness. I will have more to say about this in Part Two of the book but before we get there I want to say a little more about the interconnectedness of all things since I agree with the Kogi that a deep knowing of the reality of this interconnectedness forms the foundation of wisdom.

Slowly modern science is catching up to the Indigenous understandings of the natural world. Scientific fields as diverse as cell biology, quantum physics, ecology, and cosmology all paint a picture of the interconnectedness of everybody and everything that is deeply congruent with how the Indigenous Peoples of the world have understood it for millennia.

Entanglement and Spooky Action

In 1947, eight years before his death, Albert Einstein wrote to a friend telling him that although he could see no error in the theory of quantum mechanics that he had developed, he could not bring himself to accept one of its most troubling discoveries. He said that he felt that it was essential that physics be free from what he called, "spooky actions at a distance."[16] The spooky action he was referring to was quantum entanglement.

Quantum entanglement refers to the fact that distinct particles can be separated by time and space yet totally aligned in their behavior. What troubled Einstein was that although the particles appeared to be separate, they acted as if they were both part of a larger system that coordinated their actions. In short, quantum entanglement seemed to inescapably point to the fact that the apparent separateness was an illusion and that the fundamental reality was a profound interconnectedness.

This spooky action of quantum entanglement that bothered Einstein has now been repeatedly measured and verified. And it remains today, no less spooky. It remains inexplicable that things that are half a world apart could be deeply linked in some way that defies their apparent separateness. The notion of a butterfly flapping its wings in Asia and this having the potential to be immediately

> Slowly, modern science is catching up to the Indigenous understandings of the world.

and directly linked to some corresponding event in North America sounds beyond belief. But, scientists assure us that quantum entanglement is real.

To me, this sounds like a confirmation of not just what the Indigenous peoples of the world have been saying but also the mystics. It suggests that, in the words of the Hindu mystic Ramana Maharshi, "There are no others." Separateness may just be the world's greatest optical illusion! Regardless of how independent we perceive our actions and even our selves to be, it suggests that everyone and everything is joined together in a great cosmic dance. In Christian terms, this is the dance of our oneness in Christ with everyone and everything in existence, since to exist is to be held in Christ.[17]

Morphic Resonance

Cellular biologists also offer evidence of this same fundamental interconnectedness of everything. The work of British scientist, Rupert Sheldrake, is a good illustration of this.[18]

Sheldrake and others have demonstrated that cells have memory, this perhaps being the basis of the "evolutionary habits" that Darwin noted. Darwin puzzled over these "habits" (such things, for example, as the distinctive patterns of color on birds of the same species, or the number, shape and color of flower petals of the same species) in much the same ways as Einstein puzzled over quantum entanglement.

Cells seem to organize themselves and their growth based on attunement to each other. Sheldrake describes this attunement as morphic resonance. It operates on the basis of similarity, just as is the case in the more familiar experience of acoustic resonance. If, for example, you sing middle "C" into the strings of a piano they will vibrate back at that precise same pitch. That's resonance. Radio and television are also both resonant technologies that work in the same way when you tune into a specific frequency.

In this same way, organisms tune into others that are like them. For example, tulips are naturally attuned to other tulips, elephant seals to other elephant seals, and eagles to other eagles. DNA directs each living form to manufacture the correct proteins that enable this tuning, just like each radio station transmits on that station's specific tuning frequency. It appears that resonance tuning may well be at least part of the way plants inherit their form and animals their instincts.

The significance of this is that it demonstrates that plants and animals exist within an invisible, interconnected web of attunement. And it also demonstrates that, just as we saw in quantum entanglement, this interconnectedness transcends space and time.

Every member of a species draws upon the experience of not just other living members of the species wherever in the world they may be, but also upon the collective memory of the whole species. This is quite similar to the collective unconscious described by C. G. Jung in that it serves as the repository of the wisdom of the species. It connects all organisms within a species to each other and it does this across time and space.

Humans are also part of this web of interconnectedness and, if we are attentive, we will notice the ways in which we also experience resonance that may well influence how we act and feel. While we think our emotions and actions arise totally within our separate self, we too, just like plants and animals, possess a hard-wired attunement to others within our species.

Notice, for example, how you adjust your speech, posture, or patterns of eye contact, breathing or blinking to match those of others with whom you interact. This is usually an unconscious action that betrays the reality of resonance at the human level. Furthermore, this attunement also transcends space and time. As long as people are emotionally connected over time they come to share certain traits – even including such things as propensity to obesity, happiness and loneliness.[19]

> Humans are neither separate from each other or from the world in which we exist.

Whether we choose to participate in it or not, we are, in fact, always engaged in a synchronized dance with other humans – both the people to whom we are emotionally connected but also those separated in space and time and to whom we experience no connection whatsoever. As one commentator on this phenomenon has said, "It's like without being aware of it, we are all one organism, a heaving, swirling organism contracting the feelings and thoughts of the people around us."[20]

What arrogance humans display when we refuse to accept that we are part of the natural world. Humans are neither separate from each other or from the world in which we exist. We are bound together within a larger whole and we can never experience personal wholeness apart from embracing our place on that larger web of wholeness and belonging. Wisdom starts with knowing this foundational truth. It starts, therefore, with recognizing the optical illusion of separateness.

Pausing
to Ponder

1. In this chapter I quote the Hindu mystic, Ramana Maharshi, as saying, "There are no others," going on to suggest that separateness is the world's greatest optical illusion. How do you understand what he is saying? How do you respond to it?

2. What makes you cling to your sense of separateness? What difference would it make to your sense of self and your experience of others and the world if were true that while we may be different, we are not fundamentally separate?

Additional Readings and Things to Ponder

A helpful way to move more deeply into the science of interconnectedness is to listen to the following NPR audio podcast: https://www.npr.org/programs/invisibilia/382451600/entanglement

Lisa Randall's Dark Matter and the Dinosaurs: The Astounding Interconnectedness of the Universe (New York, NY: Ecco Press, 2015) reads like a cosmological detective story as it presents the science behind the interconnectedness of everything in existence.

7   Body Wisdom

To those who have been taught to mistrust their bodies – whether as a result of bad parenting, bad experiences or bad theology – the notion of body wisdom will sound like as much of an oxymoron as an open secret, something being seriously funny, or someone being clearly confused. For many people, body and wisdom simply do not go together.

But think for a moment about the way in which the body automatically regulates itself – something physiologists describe as homeostasis. Through sophisticated sensory, feedback, and control mechanisms, our bodies resist internal change and seek to preserve tight regulation of their most essential functions. This includes such things as fluid balance, blood oxygen and sugar levels, core body temperature, arterial blood pressure, the neuroendocrine system, gene regulation, and energy balance.[21]

All of these and more are essential to our health and our bodies exercise this critical task day in and day out, beyond our awareness. Through processes that few of us even understand, our bodies demonstrate a kind of wisdom that helps us constantly adjust to ever changing internal and external environments in order to keep us in good health.

> Our bodies are grounded in the cosmic Spirit of Wisdom.

It is easy for people to simply write this off by suggesting that the body is a complex machine that possesses levels of artificial intelligence that we have not yet learned to tap. But this misses one very important point.

If, as I suggested in Chapter 4, we can speak of ants, plants, wandering albatrosses and everything else in nature drawing on the wisdom that comes from alignment with their Source, how can we say less of the human body? Our bodies are grounded in the cosmic Spirit of Wisdom. How sad that we fail to recognize and trust this. And yet that is what we do when we fail to listen to our bodies.

The notion of listening to our bodies has, of course, become something of a cliché. It's not that learning to attend to our bodies isn't important. The problem is that the motivation to do anything about it is seldom sufficient for most people to overcome the inertia associated with their denial and minimization of what their bodies are screaming at them.

The fact that we overeat even when we are aware of feeling stuffed, or that we ignore the symptoms of burnout and just keep trying to push through whatever we are facing tell us that we are usually aware of the messages our body is offering. We simply choose to ignore them. Messages about care of our bodies are, of course, ignored at our peril. But, until a person is truly motivated to do something about it, clichéd advice will never be of any value.

But, the wisdom of the body goes well beyond this first level associated with our physical well being. And, in my experience, it's important to start with the point at which motivation exists. Often this is related to the way in which the body serves as a mirror for the soul and for the spirit. And frequently I find that people are more motivated to start the work of cultivating a relationship with their bodies for psychological and spiritual reasons.

Body and Soul

Sigmund Freud described dreams as the royal road to the unconscious, suggesting that they had a singularly important role in gaining access to the depths of our psyche.[22] He was right, and I will have more to say more about dreams in the next chapter. But it wasn't long until others in the early days of psychoanalysis began to point to other royal roads to the depths of the soul – paths that were even more direct and easier to navigate.

Wilhelm Reich was an Austrian physician and psychoanalyst who was convinced that Freud had failed to appreciate the importance of the body and that it, not dreams, was the most important screen on which the issues of the soul were projected.

Reich's central concept was what he called muscular armour – that is, the way in which personality and psychopathology are reflected in the way the body moves. In his book, *Character Analysis*,[23] he argued that the body not only stores the somatic residue of our unresolved history of trauma but that its unconscious muscular habits support our character structure. The body is, therefore, the first line of defense against the aspects of our experience which we wish to deny or eliminate and the way these things are stored in our muscles shapes and reflects the deepest structures of our personality.

Now we encounter the possibility that our chronic headaches may not simply reflect stress but the overreliance on mental ways of relating to life – they may, in fact, represent an invitation to pay more attention to our hearts and souls. Or, perhaps our chronic upset stomachs are not simply a response to an as-yet unidentified food allergy but a long-term result of repressed conflicts that we continue to stuff down each time they arise.

> Deep knowing of our selves will always require deep knowing of our bodies.

Reich's insights were a major influence on Anna Freud's understanding of the ego and its mechanisms of defense[24] and through her, retain a permanent place in the contemporary psychoanalysis. They were, however, much more influential in other body psychotherapies such as primal therapy,[25] gestalt therapy,[26] and bioenergetic analysis.[27] Each offered their own tools to engage the body and tap into its wisdom but each retained Reich's insight that deep knowing of our selves will always require deep knowing of our bodies.

Body and Spirit

Body work approaches that help people connect to their minds and souls have become common in the West in the last 50 years. In addition to those that I have already mentioned, these include approaches such as Bowenwork,[28] Rolfing,[29] the Alexander Technique,[30] and Tragerwork,[31] to name but a few. But, for the most part, they neglect the role of the spirit. In contrast, the East has long emphasized body work as a connection to spirit, although often these approaches neglect the soul.

There are, however, a few approaches to bodywork that are truly holistic – emphasizing the way in which the body serves as an important means of connecting to both soul and spirit. Of these, the one that is undoubtedly the most developed is one with which I have limited personal experience. However, I know enough of it to have great respect for it. It is the chakra system that was first developed in India over four thousand years ago and continues to be developed and widely practice in both the East and the West.

> If the outer word is to be engaged with wisdom the process must begin within.

The chakras are energy centers in the body, each of which has it's own purpose and makes it own contribution to the unfolding of the human journey. But while they are situated within, they point to that which is beyond, serving as what, in Yoga philosophy, is thought of as a set of portals between the inner and outer worlds. These outer worlds that exist beyond the self include not just the physical world, but also the spiritual world. And, as Yoga practice and philosophy reminds us, if the outer world is to be engaged with wisdom the process must begin within.

The chakra system is both a map of the universe and a map of the human evolutionary journey – showing not just what lies behind us but also what spiritually lies ahead of us. In psychological terms, it addresses issues of love and relationship, power and spirituality, emotion and instinct, thinking and intuition. In the words of Anodea Judith, it "maps . . . the body through the human nervous system . . . the psyche through developmental stages of childhood . . . (and) the spiritual quest through states of consciousness."[32]

There are seven chakras stacked in a column of energy that spans from the base of the spine to the top of the head. Graphically, these can be represented as follows:[33]

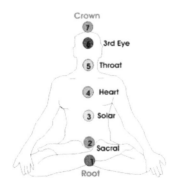

Each of the chakras is associated with a state of consciousness and together represent the way in which the evolutionary life force runs through the vertical axis of humans. The lower chakras are primarily related to such practical matters as survival, movement, and action. The higher chakras are associated with the psychological and spiritual dimensions of life.

By way of summary, here are the major issues associated with each of these energy centers:

Chakra	Associated with Core Issues of
1. Root	Survival, money and food
2. Sacral	Sexuality and our connections with others
3. Solar Plexus	Power and control of our lives
4. Heart	Love, joy and inner peace
5. Throat	Communication and self expression
6. Third Eye	Intuition and imagination
7. Crown	Cognition and integrated spirituality

Chakra work helps people move both up and down through these energy centers. As taught by Anodea Judith, author of one of the most helpful introductions to chakra work I am familiar with, downward movement follows the pull of the body and soul and moves us toward individuality. Upward movement, on the other hand, is a response to the pull of mind and spirit and moves us toward universality.[34] Downward movement is the path of manifestation and immanence. Upward movement is the path of liberation and transcendence. Both lead to the Divine and both, therefore, are paths of access to the Spirit of Wisdom.

Humans need to make both these journeys and need to maintain a balance in the work we do on each. This is totally consistent with my own mapping of human unfolding and what I have described as the journey from body to mind to soul and to spirit. As I have argued in my book, *Spirituality and the Awakening Self*, we need to move both up and down this chain of being in order to become fully integrated and whole.[35]

Chakra work is not the only way to engage with our bodies in a way that supports both our psychological and spiritual journey. I mention it, however, because it comes from a rich and ancient wisdom tradition that has much to offer if what you seek is healing and wholeness of body, soul and spirit.

Pausing
to Ponder

1. *How in touch with your body are you? What messages from it are you most prone to ignore? What, if anything, invites you to a deeper knowing of your body and the wisdom it can help you access?*

2. *Think about the primary thrust of your own journey, whether it represents primarily a journey toward spirit or a journey toward your body. What keeps you from paying more attention to the journey you most tend to ignore?*

Additional Readings and Things to Ponder

A very practical and helpful resource for body-soul work is David E. Sobel and Robert E. Ornstein, *Mind & Body Health Handbook: How to Use Your Mind & Body to Relieve Stress, Overcome Illness, and Enjoy Healthy Pleasures, 2nd Edition* (Los Altos, CA: DRx, 1996).

The book about chakra work that I mentioned in this chapter is Anodea Judith, *Eastern Body, Western Mind* (New York, NY: Celestial Arts, 2004).

8   Unconscious Wisdom

We ended the last chapter with the reminder that the journey of human unfolding is never simply a journey of ascent. It must also necessarily involve descent. Both movements are essential as each deepens and enriches the other. Wisdom can only be accessed when both phases of this cycle are embraced.

One of the great mysteries of human existence is the flowing interaction between the conscious and unconscious realms of life. And once again, wisdom turns up where we might least expect to find it – not just in the illumination of consciousness but in the darkness of the unconscious.

> Authentic movement toward wisdom starts by tapping into the inner wisdom that resides at the core of our being.

The psyche is dynamically alive and participates in the eternal dance between consciousness and the unconscious. Consciousness cannot exist without the sustaining presence of the unconscious. And it can never evolve or be transformed apart from openness to the unconscious.

Expansion of consciousness comes through increased access to the unconscious. The point of this access is not to do battle with the unconscious in an attempt to tame or subdue it. The reason this access is so important is that it allows us to draw on its wisdom and subsequently live with more vitality, creativity, freedom and fullness of being.

Any genuine movement to wholeness and increased wisdom must involve tapping into the inner wisdom that exists at the core of our being as this brings us into direct contact with the cosmic Spirit of Wisdom that is the foundation of everything in existence. But notice the direction of movement – down and into the particular and personal (our unconscious) leading us up and out to the cosmic and transpersonal (Consciousness and the cosmic Spirit of Wisdom).

Befriending Your Unconscious

The first step to becoming better acquainted with your unconscious is to recognize just how different its operating system is from that of consciousness.

The language of consciousness is built around words, reason, and propositions. In contrast, the language of the unconscious is built around images, myths, symbols and archetypes. The psychology of each, therefore, is profoundly different. Whereas consciousness strives for order, clarity, coherence, and meaning, the unconscious refuses to be tamed and thrives in what, from the perspective of consciousness, appears to be disorder, impulsivity and chaos. And whereas consciousness is serious, the unconscious is more playful and provocative. It's no wonder that on first encounter, the unconscious is often, at the best, bewildering, and at the worst, terrifying!

Don't set out to analyze or even understand your unconscious. That's an unrealistic task and an unhelpful goal. Approach the befriending of your depths with something more like the posture of a curious explorer. Notice what appears at the edges of consciousness, or in times of daydreaming, falling asleep, fantasy or dreams. Don't judge what you observe or try to fix or eliminate it. Hold whatever you encounter lightly and without judgment, receiving it with hospitality, playfulness and imagination. And be attentive to the images, memories and feelings that arise in you as you do. Don't push them. Just give them room to breathe and develop in the light of your conscious engagement with them.

But let us now turn to the question of how to unpack the wisdom of what is probably the most accessible product of the unconscious – our dreams.

The Wisdom of Dreams

Prior to eighteenth century most people assumed dreams had spiritual significance. The earliest recorded dreams reveal that they were received as messages from the gods or encounters with the spirits of gods themselves.[36] Indigenous societies around the world continue to view them in spiritual terms and treat dreams in similar ways. Usually they are understood to be a cosmic doorway into another dimension of reality that offers individuals an opportunity to open their spiritual eyes so they can receive gifts, not just for them as individuals and their community.

Dreams often play a central role in whatever coming of age vision quest rituals mark the young person's readiness to take as adults within traditional or Indigenous communities. For example, the Gullah Geechee (African Americans who continue to speak the Gullah language of West Africa and preserve their traditional culture) of the costal regions of Georgia and South Carolina, continue to bring their dreams to a daily community meeting where, with the counsel of the elders, they seek to discern the gifts of each dream for the community. Young people are granted the right to join this daily meeting of the adults when they have completed their "seekin" coming of age ritual that includes spending as many days as is needed alone in the marshy grasslands until they have a dream that offers such gifts.

> Dreams offer access to greater self-awareness, creativity and insight into the existential challenges and spiritual potentials of human life.

The Gullah are not alone in recognizing that not all dreams are alike. The reason for this is that dreams serve a number of quite different psychological functions.[37] While they recognize that all dreams have value for the individual, only the special, less common but not infrequent ones are given to the individual for the community. Their deep reliance on the wisdom of these special dreams is the reason communal dream work is so central to their culture.

Current dream research is also beginning to recognize the way in which dreams allow us to access the wisdom of the unconscious. Dr. Kelly Bulkeley, a dream researcher and director of an open-access online sleep and dream database of over 30,000 dream reports, describes dreams as connecting the dreamer with something greater than him or herself, something more powerful and wiser.[38] Speaking of the wisdom that dreams represent, he describes dreams as a neurologically hard-wired avenue of access to "greater self-awareness, creativity, and insight into the existential challenges and spiritual potentials of human life."[39]

Showing Hospitality to Dreams

I used to describe engagement with our dreams as work. I now prefer to think of it as an act of hospitality. The notion of work sets us up to try and interpret or make something of the dream. In contrast, reminding ourselves that the basic task in engaging with our dreams is to receive them with hospitality releases us from our instrumental and transactional agendas and invites us to simply be present to them.

Treat your dreams as a treasured guest in the home of your self. Make no demands of them and by all means, avoid trying to force them into some pre-conceived framework or co-op them to some agenda. Just be with them in openness, curiosity and respect, and then be attentive to the gifts that come from such a sacred encounter.

Think of the dream as a parable or a Zen koan, and avoid taking it literally. Treat each symbol you encounter (each person, each object, each action) as representing some part of your self – not simply your conscious self but more importantly the self you do not know. But keep your focus on the overall dream and the overall message it brings.

Rather than asking questions of the dream (i.e., "I wonder why I dreamed about her?" or, "What on earth does that mean?") allow the dream to ask questions of you.

For example, a couple of nights ago I dreamt I was sailing a large yacht without any crew and suddenly found myself in a storm with raging winds that were tearing the sails faster than I could manage to lower and stow them. Far from being obscure, this dream reflects a situation I have been in several times while sailing but more importantly, a theme that has frequently appeared in my dreams with other symbolic packaging. But, my unconscious recognized that once again I needed to hear the warning it carried and so it offered me this dream.

Reflecting on this dream was easy because it was relatively transparent. It contained none of the disguise that the most important dreams usually display. But as I reflected on it, here are several of the questions I noted in my dream journal the next morning:

1. What aspects of my life are out of control?

2. What personal responsibilities am I ignoring and instead projecting onto others who fail to meet my expectation to turn up to take care of me?
3. What invitations to deeper engagement with community may this dream be inviting me to consider?

Don't feel you need to get these questions right or try to squeeze from the dream all the potentially important questions it might offer. Dreams are incredibly redundant. If you are paying attention to them and to your unconscious, each night you will receive just exactly what you need for the present moment of your life. If you miss something, your unconscious will raise it again. Eventually it will stop doing this if you continue to ignore the messages. However, if you are hospitably attentive to your dreams and your inner life, your unconscious will recognize this and offer you increasingly rich gifts. It all starts with hospitable attention.

This is, of course, only the first level of engagement with dreams. There is much, much more to be learned and good resources available to help you do so. Remember, however, that the dreamer is always the best person to recognize and receive the gifts of the unconscious. I have worked with both my own dreams and those of others for over forty years but have never told anyone what their dream means. So, avoid books or people who are eager to tell you what your dreams and their symbols mean. There is an important role for learning more about symbolic language but save your engagement with that until you have practiced dream hospitality as I describe it above for an extended time.

And don't forget the wisdom of Indigenous and traditional societies. They know that although the dreamer has the first responsibility to hospitably receive the dream, the deepest levels of significance of dreams usually requires sharing and holding them with others.

You don't need a whole community to do this. My wife and I have shared our significant dreams over breakfast for the past 5 decades. Spiritual directors and psychotherapists are also potentially good resources that are often available. As are good friends who you trust and who understand that their role is not to do anything more than hold your dreams with you as you explore the gifts they offer.

Pausing
to Ponder

1. *What, if any, invitations do you hear in reading this chapter to begin to try and befriend your unconscious? What concrete steps can you take to move in the direction your heart is calling you? What will be the biggest obstacles that you will need to overcome in moving in this direction?*

Additional Readings and Things to Ponder

Recall that I said in this chapter that, along with images, myths and symbols are the primary language of the unconscious. If you want to learn more about myths and symbols, Joseph Campbell is an incomparable resource.

If you are not familiar with his work, start with any of the many video recording of his lectures and interviews that are available on the Internet. YouTube alone has 57 of these videos, totally over 8 hours of material. One of my favorites remains the 6-part series of conversations with Bill Moyers done for PBS. In North America this is currently available on Netflix, packaged as *Joseph Campbell and the Power of Myth, with Bill Moyers*. If you are unable to access this on chances are good you can still find it somewhere on the Internet or broadcast outlet.

Once you have encountered Joseph Campbell on video you can then read any of his books that call to your heart when you look at the list of them that is easily accessed on the Internet. I would recommend starting with either *The Hero with a Thousand Faces* (Novato, CA: New World Library, 2008) or *The Power of Myth*, written with Bill Moyers (New York, NY: Anchor, 1991). But, start with anything that draws your heart. Spend a season immersing yourself in the wisdom of this man and you will never be the same again!

My personal approach to engaging dreams is an eclectic one, drawing heavily on Jung but also Freud and Fritz Pearls (Founder of Gestalt Therapy). However, people tell me there are quite unique elements in in my approach that are not found in any of the more major dream work traditions. Learn more about the way I engage dreams in Appendix 1 of *Spirituality and the Awakening Self* (Grand Rapids, MI: Brazos, 2012) where I offer the fullest discussion of dreams.

One final, crucially important resource if you wish to better understand and learn how to cultivate a relationship with your unconscious is the work of Carl Jung. An excellent starting point for this is Joseph Campbell's *Portable Jung* (New York, NY: Penguin Classics, 1976). This isn't a book about Jung but a collection of some of his most important essays. After reading it I'd suggest Jung's autobiography, *Memories, Dreams, Reflections* (New York, NY: Vantage Books, 1989).

9   Perennial Wisdom

I have always been drawn to the big-picture view of things. If some people climb mountains simply because they are there, I am always pulled toward summits by the promise of an ever expanding vista. There is simply nothing like a macro perspective on life to help me live on the micro level at which life comes at me.

This, to me, has always been the attraction of the perennial wisdom tradition (sometimes referred to as the perennial tradition, or, perennial philosophy). To someone who is hardwired to seek big-picture perspective on life, an encounter with this ancient and continuing tradition is like leading a child into a candy store! But because it is a stretch for most of us to think of philosophy as candy, let's talk about this tradition in terms that are more descriptive of what it truly is.

The perennial wisdom tradition is a compilation of the deep sources of wisdom that have shaped human culture and that form the common core of the world's major religions – Christianity included. This does not mean that the distinctives of the religious traditions it draws on are unimportant. Christianity is not the same as Sufism, Islam the same as Baha'ism, or Taoism the same as Hinduism. The distinctives allow each separate tradition to speak with its own voice and tell its own story, but the common core allows us to hear that story in broader and deeper terms.

As a Christian, I find it encouraging that there is such a significant shared core to these various wisdom traditions. I find it helps me understand my own tradition when I encounter it in the light of the spiritual wisdom that is quite easily found if one considers even the contours of the perennial tradition. And that is what I propose to do – simply look at the contours of this common core of wisdom. For even those, I think we will see, are enough to help us ground ourselves in, and align ourselves with, a reality that is vastly grander than what we usually realize.

All spiritual and religious traditions have something to say about four important matters: the nature of ultimate reality, the possibilities of human knowing of this ultimate reality, the nature of personhood, and the goal of human existence. In what follows, I will draw together some of the central insights of the perennial wisdom tradition associated with each of these four areas and conclude with several important consequences for living that are suggested by them.[40]

Ultimate Reality

However named, God is the Ultimate Reality. Language does not serve well to describe this Ultimate Reality since it is so profoundly supra-human and trans-personal. Yet, humans need to name things and so across time and the various wisdom traditions we have adopted such linguistic handles as the Spirit of Wisdom, Divine Presence, The Wholly Other, The One, The Ground of Being, or God. All names for this foundation of existence point to the same reality – a reality that, at the same time, is both transcendent and immanent, not set apart from the world of humans and things but deeply connected to everything that is.

> Ultimate Reality will always lie beyond the fingers of our images and concepts that we use to point toward it.

All names for Ultimate Reality fail miserably in the task of capturing it. How easily we forget that language does not hold reality; at its best it just points toward it. Our problem, however, is that we confuse our puny construals with the reality to which they, even at their best, point.

Anthony de Mello tells a one-sentence story from the perennial wisdom tradition that nicely illustrates this.

> The master encouraged his followers to look at the moon by pointing toward it but noticed that his followers inevitably looked at his finger, not the moon.[41]

The story tells us that Ultimate Reality will always lie beyond all the fingers of our images and concepts that we use to point toward it. We must, therefore, be ever vigilant in realizing the danger of getting stuck in our words and concepts rather than getting in touch with the reality behind them. This is true in all of life, but nowhere more true than when we use words to point toward the Wholly Other that is Ultimate Reality.

Ultimate Reality is the source, substance and sustenance of all that is. Nothing exists without it. To be removed from this vital connection would be to instantly cease to exist. We exist because we are in relation to Ultimate Reality, or more precisely, because we exist within it.

The Possibility of Ultimate Knowing

> We only truly know that with which we become one. Communion is knowing through union.

This raises, however, a crucial question. If this assertion about the nature of Ultimate Reality is to have any meaning for us, it must be knowable in some way. The mystics of the Perennial Wisdom Tradition assert that direct, immediate knowing is possible. They tell us that such knowing is not based on reason nor deduction but on communion.

We only truly know that with which we become one. Communion is knowing through union. Knowing God means, therefore union with God – something that the mystics have always proclaimed to be not just possible but the goal and fulfilment of humanity.

Knowing is, therefore, becoming one with that which we seek to know. We see this in the Hebrew Bible's use of the language of knowing to describe sexual intercourse (as in "Adam knew Eve"). Knowing is intimate and this intimacy is transformational. We come to resemble that which we know. The more we resemble that which we seek to know, the more we truly know it, and the more truly we know it the more we are one with it.

Union is not sameness but likeness. However, in union, the dualism that initially separates subsequently dissolves and we experience the unity that holds us both. This is, of course, a profound mystery – a mystery that lies beyond understanding but not beyond the possibility of experiential knowing.

The Mystery of Personhood

The possibility of human knowing of Ultimate Reality is grounded in the fact that humans are a reflection of this reality that is remarkably similar to its source. All personal knowing is based in likeness. We can only truly know that which we already resemble in some important way. This possibility lies in the human soul where we retain traces of our origin. In other words, the ground of our being is the Ground of Being.

This brings us right to the core of the mystery of human personhood. Humans are especially connected to Ultimate Reality because, in some mysterious way, the human soul contains something similar to, possibly even identical with, the Ultimate Reality we name as God. Humans are a unique expression of this reality.

The depths of the human soul mirror the depths of Spirit. There is a place in the depths of our soul in which Ultimate Reality alone can dwell and in which we dwell in Ultimate Reality. Meister Eckhart says that "the nameless depth in me cries out to the nameless depth in God" – our profound human mystery crying out to the divine mystery beyond names, forms and distinctions that is our source and ground.

To be – as described in the Christian tradition – made in the image of Ultimate Mystery, means that humans will inevitably be a fundamental mystery to themselves. Human mystery is an echo of Ultimate Reality. The key to knowing human mystery is knowing Ultimate Reality. And the key to knowing the mystery of Ultimate Reality, is meeting that Reality in the depths of the human soul.

The Goal of Human Existence

In every cell of their being the deepest human longing is to know the source and ground of our existence. This, the Perennial Wisdom Tradition teaches, is the goal and meaning of being human. Life has a direction. All of life flows from and returns to Divine Presence. Our Origin is our Destiny! So, as the river said to the seeker, "Does one really have to fret about the journey? No matter which way I turn, I'm homeward bound!"

Once again, words do a very poor job of describing this direction of the flow of human life. In the Christian tradition we speak of union with the Divine – sometimes daring to adopt the even bolder language of *theosis*, or divinization. Take, for example, the words spoken by the priest when mixing the water and the wine in the Roman Catholic mass – "By the mystery of this water and wine may we come to share in the divinity of Christ who humbled himself to share in our humanity." Union with Ultimate Reality is sharing the divinity of Christ. It is participating in the Divine Presence. This is the fulfillment of humanity.

Consequences for Living

Many things flow from an appreciation of the fact that the purpose of life is this unitive knowing of the ground of our being. When identified primarily with our bodies, minds, experience or any lesser thing, we lack full awareness of our spiritual nature and the truth of the ground of our being. The moral of the perennial wisdom tradition is "Don't settle for anything less than the truth of your Christ-self." The ego-self with which we are all much more familiar is a small cramped place when compared with the spaciousness of our true self-in-Christ. This is the self that is not only one within itself, it is at one with the world and all others who share it as their world. It is, therefore, one with Ultimate Reality.

> Don't settle for anything less than the truth of your Christ-self.

Life, therefore, is a constant flow of invitations to awaken to these spiritual realities. Spiritual practices are, at their best, cooperation with life's inherent tendency toward spiritual awakening and unfolding – a tendency that Christians name as grace. Awakening is the expression of that grace in which we see through our apparent separation and notice that we are already one with Divine Presence and with all that is. All that is missing is awareness.

> *Pausing*
>
> *to Ponder*

1. Christians are sometimes nervous about learning from other religious traditions. This is surprising given the Biblical assertion that Jesus is the light that enlightens all humans (John 1: 9) and that God has left evidence of the Divine Self in all cultures and religions (Acts 14: 17). How do you make sense of the wisdom that God has left evident to other cultures and religions?

2. Reflect for a moment on the four central principles that are common to all of the world's major religions, and the implications I draw from them. What, to you, are the major implications of these four foundational spiritual insights? What difference might they make to your life if you lived on the basis of their truth?

Additional Readings and Things to Ponder

The term "Perennial Philosophy" was coined by Leibniz, but popularized by Aldous Huxley. The classic work on this ancient wisdom tradition is Aldous Huxley's book entitled *The Perennial Philosophy* (New York, NY: Harper Perennial Modern Classics, 2009), originally published in 1945 and continuously in print since then.

10   Mystical Wisdom

Many Christians find the mystics, perhaps I can say, somewhat mystifying. Their language often makes it hard to identify with them and the popular image of the solitary mystic in the woods or monastery suggests that they are profoundly out of sync with the modern world.

It is easy, therefore, to think of mysticism as relevant only to spiritual gurus or those trying to escape mainstream life. This would, however, be a tragic mistake because the mystics are remarkably relevant to modern life and have an enormously important contribution to make to understanding and living wisdom.

However, before we attempt to learn from this rich Christian tradition let me take a moment to clear some common misconceptions.

The Mystical Core of Christian Spirituality

Despite what you might have heard, Christian mysticism is not about seeing visions or receiving special messages from God. Nor is it the pursuit of esoteric spiritual or religious experiences. Mysticism is simply the longing for heart knowing of God.

Immature spirituality focuses on experience. Mature spirituality focuses on seeing and knowing. And this is what the most mature of the mystics offer us. Their words and their life reflect a deep, stabilized knowing of Ultimate Reality. Rather than being satisfied with beliefs, they teach us how to actually know, not just know *about*, God.

Christian mysticism is participation in the mystery of the transformational journey toward union with God in love.[42] The pursuit of visions, raptures or other high-octane experiences is simply a dangerous distraction from this journey.

Union with God in love is the mystical core of the Christian spiritual

> Mystics long to know God in love and be filled with the fullness of God.

journey. Recall St. Paul's prayer in which he asks that you might know that, "planted in love and built on love, you, with all the saints, will be able to grasp the breadth and the length, the height and the depth of God's love; until, knowing fully the love of Christ which is beyond all knowledge, you are filled with the utter fullness of God."[43]

A mystic is simply a person who longs for this knowing of the fullness of God. Perhaps this includes you. I know it includes me.

Mystics are defined more by their longing than by their experience. They long to know God in love and be filled with the fullness of God. They receive this longing as God's longing flowing into and through them – something that they come to realize is true of all creation. They come to know this as they learn to see through the eyes of Christ and know through the heart and mind of Christ. And the wisdom they have to offer us is wisdom that is associated with the journey into the heart of knowing God in love.

What Mystics Know

Everyone has had momentary experiences of the larger transcendent realities that form the horizon of human existence but most of us fail to notice them. And when we do, we quickly allow them to slip from consciousness.

Mystics live with a profound awareness of the fact that everything in existence is sacred because it is held in Christ. Knowing this, not simply believing it, is the basis of their stabilized background awareness of the web of interconnected belonging that holds them and everything else in existence.

Here are just a few of the many other things the mystics know:

- Mystics know that everything belongs because everything is a manifestation of the Infinite Presence that is God.

- Mystics know that this Infinite Presence is, moment by moment, birthing itself as our presence and as the presence of all things.

- Mystics know that this makes them and all of us siblings to everything in existence.

- Mystics know that the language of the spiritual journey is somewhat misleading because there is, in reality, nowhere to go and nothing to achieve. They know that God is already present and we already exist in God and God in us. All that is lacking is awareness.

⚜ Mystics also know that it is possible for all of us to know the things they know. They are witnesses to the possibility of living with a stable, deep knowing of the reality of our being in God and God's being in us.[44]

Mature mystics do not simply tell what they know. Nor do they focus on the experiences that may have played a part in their knowing. They speak and live in a way that allows us to experience a deep resonance with what they know. For many of us, this is the beginning of the way in which their knowing becomes our knowing.

Mystics do not so much see God as they see life through the eyes of God. They live the reality that Meister Eckhart describes when he says, "The eye with which I see God is the same eye with which He sees me. Mine eye and God's eye are one eye and one sight and one knowledge and one love."[45] All mystical seeing and knowing emerges from the radical truth of our being in Christ. This is why seeing through the eyes of Christ and knowing through the mind and heart of Christ is the basis of wisdom.

How Mystics Know

But *how* the mystics know the things they know is at least as important as *what* they know.

Mystical knowing is beyond reason, but not irrational. It is trans-rational. It involves a new level of knowing that is made possible by means of transformed consciousness. It is personal, not objective. What the mystics know they know with the totality of their being, not merely with their minds.

The sixteenth century Spanish mystic, John of the Cross, says that God cannot be thought but can be loved. By this he meant that God cannot be grasped by the mind but can be known by the heart. The route to this heart knowing is contemplation. This is because contemplation (or meditation) holds unique potential to help us to transcend our minds without abandoning them.

> Love is its own form of knowing. We know what we love and what we love we also know.

We can, therefore, describe mystical knowing as contemplative knowing. Contemplation is apprehension that is uncluttered by thought – particularly preconception and analysis. It is based on direct personal encounter. When you know something by means of such encounter you may not be able to express it verbally – at least not in a compelling, coherent or exhaustive manner. But, you know that you know because your knowing has a depth and immediacy to it that is never present in simply knowing *about* things – even merely knowing *about* God.

Knowing God who is love will always involve knowing God *in love* or *through love*. Love is its own form of knowing. Real knowing is always deeply personal and intimate. We know what we love and what we love we also know.

Contemplation isn't thinking about something or other – even thinking about God. It is making space in our hearts for the touch of the Loving and Living God, and then allowing that touch to flow through the rest of our being and out into the world.

This sort of knowing is not something that is only available to certain types of people. In fact, it has nothing whatsoever to do with personality. The awakening of our hearts and learning to bring the mind down into the heart that I will describe in much more detail in later chapters is something that we can all experience. Without this awakening, none of us has any hope of accessing the deep wisdom that the mystics tell us comes from our being in Christ.

Wisdom is built on a foundation of living with deep, abiding awareness of being in Christ. With this foundation we then come to know, not just believe, that everything in existence comes from, is sustained by, and is flowing back into God for its wholeness. This is the basis of the sacred interconnectedness of all things that is the foundation of wisdom. And this is the core of mystical knowing and the wisdom that flows from it.

> *Pausing*
>
> *to Ponder*

1. *Which of the things mystics know, and tell us we also can know, touched your heart in a way that made you say, "I wish I could know that?" Which of these knowings have you sensed but have not yet become stable parts of your background awareness?*

2. *What do you know in your heart that could never be reduced to reason or words? Notice how certain you can be of this knowing even though it is irreducible to logic or the senses. This is heart or contemplative knowing.*

3. *Notice how again we have encountered this theme of the interconnectedness of all things. What do you know of this reality? When have you sensed yourself to be deeply connected to the earth, or deeply woven within the fabric of humanity – not just part of your tribe? What implications for your way of being in the world might you suspect would flow from a deep, knowing of these things?*

Additional Readings and Things to Ponder

Pick a mystic that you have always wanted to read and read something
by him or her. If you are unsure where to start, Carl McColman,
Christian Mystics: 108 Seers, Saints and Sages (Hampton Roads,
Newburyport, MA: 2016) offers a wonderful introduction to the most
important Christian mystics and an excellent way of engaging them and
their wisdom.

For a more in-depth but secondary source discussion of the wisdom of
the mystics I would recommend Peter N. Borys, Jr., *Transforming Heart
and Mind: Learning from the Mystics* (New York: Paulist Press, 2006).

11   Sapiential Christianity

We have already anonymously encountered the Christian wisdom
tradition in Chapter 1 when I described the importance of the heart in
accessing wisdom, and in the last chapter when we discussed the gifts
of the Christian mystics. In his review of Sapiential Christianity, Bruno
Barnhart suggests that it is the mystics and monastics who have
preserved and passed this tradition of knowing through the heart on to
us.[46] However, the gifts of this tradition are far from restricted to
mystics and monastics and it is those gifts I want to unpack in this
chapter.

The starting point in understanding the Christian wisdom tradition is
Jesus who Cynthia Bourgeault describes as first and foremost a wisdom
master and teacher. In her
book, *The Wisdom Jesus*, she
states that regardless of how
else we have come to think of
Jesus after-the-fact, in first-
century Palestine it is clear that
the people who encountered
him would have recognized him
to be a *moshel moshelim*, or a
teacher of wisdom.[47]

A wisdom teacher is someone who teaches the path of inner transformation.

Wisdom teachers were common
throughout the East and Middle
East and held an important role
within Judaism. The authors of such Hebrew wisdom literature as

Ecclesiastes, Job and Proverbs were wisdom teachers and early precursors of the modern Jewish Rabbi – and if you have any doubt that Jesus was part of this tradition, recall that those who encountered him instinctively addressed him as "Rabbi."

A wisdom teacher was someone who taught the path of inner transformation. This path was such a central part of the religions of the Middle East that it was a natural part of the heritage of both Judaism and Christianity.

The Christianity of the West has always been what Bourgeault calls "savior-oriented" – this expressing itself in a focus on *Soteriology, or the* path to salvation. In contrast, the Christianity of the East has always been "wisdom oriented," the emphasis in Eastern Christianity being on *Sophiology,* or the path to inner transformation and living wisdom. Bourgeault draws out the implication of this:

> Whatever theological premises you may or may not choose to believe about Jesus, the primary task of a Christian is not to believe theological premises but to put on the mind of Christ.[48]

This acquisition of a new consciousness that Christians describe as the mind of Christ is the core of the inner transformation that is involved in accessing wisdom. Because it is so central to Sapiential Christianity we will look much more closely at what this involves in Chapter 16.

Two central features of the teaching of Jesus make clear that he was a wisdom teacher. The first was his emphasis on the heart. The second was his use of parables. These two are not separate but a single feature of wisdom teaching. Both were designed to side-step the mind and speak directly to the heart. Both were designed to demonstrate the limitations of normal mental processes in accessing Truth and to facilitate the awakening of the heart and enlightenment of the whole being.

If Jesus had wanted to simply transmit knowledge or teach beliefs he would have spoken in a much more direct, propositional manner. Instead, his speech was full of paradox and puzzling statements that he refused to explain. This was because his goal was the acquisition of a new mind, a new consciousness, a totally new way of being.

Barnhart describes the core of the Christian sapiential tradition in these words:

> Sapiential Christianity is not a body of knowledge but a way of knowing. It is a way of knowing that engages not only intellect, but mind, heart, soul, and body: our fully enfleshed humanity. It is the way of knowing that opens when one listens with the ear of the heart.[49]

Wisdom is a mode of consciousness. We could also describe it as experiential knowing. But because faith is the fundamental way of knowing, it is faith in knowing in darkness. I will return to this central role of faith in more details in Chapter 15 where we will see that the faith that receives emphasis in Sapiential Christianity is not faith-as-beliefs but faith-as-trust. It is trust that we need if we are to walk the transformational wisdom path. Beliefs simply are not up to the task.

In his review of the history and theology of Sapiential Christianity, Barnhart notes that wisdom consciousness is central to the New

Testament and remained the dominant mode of theological understanding in both the Eastern and Western Christian traditions for more than twelve centuries.[50] This changed in the twelfth through fifteenth centuries with the rise of what would later be called scholasticism or rationalism – the mind gradually replacing the heart as the center of knowing and wisdom being replaced with beliefs.

This is why the Christian wisdom tradition is so unfamiliar to most contemporary Christians. What I suspect would first come to mind if someone asked them about the Christian wisdom tradition would be the short, pithy sayings of the Book of Proverbs. In simple practical language, these proverbs teach things like avoiding gossip and laziness, valuing prudence and moderation, and being diligent in work. Reading like a summary of practical ethics or morality what they offer is more the fruit of wisdom than wisdom itself. Taken as a list of things to do and avoid doing, they could mistakenly suggest that wisdom is something we can achieve with sufficient effort. But wisdom is not just following good advice. It is something much more personal. In fact, it is a person.

Wisdom Personified

We see this in the fact that repeatedly, in Proverbs and throughout the Wisdom literature of the Bible, wisdom is personified. Her voice – and she is consistently presented as female[51] - is at the center of Biblical wisdom literature.

According to Proverbs 8:22, "Lady Wisdom" (as she is sometimes known) was God's first creation. This takes us back before the first chapter of the Bible itself, before God said, "Let there be light." In the very beginning, Wisdom appears on the scene as the first manifestation of God.

In the Book of Proverbs Wisdom often addresses us in the first person singular. Listen to her speak:

> Yahweh created me . . . from everlasting, I was firmly set, from the beginning, before the earth came into being . . . When he traced the foundations of the earth, I was beside the master craftsman, delighting him day after day, ever at play in his presence.[52]

Clearly, Wisdom is nothing less than the Divine Presence – with God from the beginning.

As you might suspect from its name, the Book of Wisdom describes her most fully.[†] Here Wisdom is described as the fashioner of all things, the breath of the power of God, a pure emanation of the glory of the Almighty, a reflection of eternal light, a spotless mirror of the working of God, and an image of God's goodness.[53]

[†] Unfortunately, the parts of the Bible where Wisdom presents herself most fully are the parts of the Bible that Protestants generally do not read – the Apocrypha (meaning, things that are hidden). Roman Catholics, Anglicans/Episcopalians and Eastern Orthodox Christians consider these the Apocryphal Books to be deuterocanonical (that is, of secondary authority), but still important to be read. Protestants have nothing to fear in doing so.

This same Wisdom who was beside the master craftsman at creation was also placed by God in the depths of the human soul by God as an inner light.[54] She is also present throughout creation – available to everything in existence. She possesses all knowledge and truth and is the foundation of good judgment and government.[55] No wonder she is more precious than sapphires or jewels.[56] No wonder nothing else is more worthy of desire than her.[57]

So, we might wonder, where can we find this jewel of inestimable value? The Book of Wisdom answers this question quite clearly.

> By those who love her, Wisdom is readily seen; by those who seek her, she is readily found. Wisdom anticipates those who desire her by making herself known. Whoever gets up early to find her will have no trouble but will discover her sitting at the door as she herself searches everywhere for those who seek her, benevolently appearing to them on their way.[58]

I am not a Biblical scholar, but reading those who are, I am led to the inescapable conclusion that Wisdom is the feminine personification of God. In the words of Bruce Sanguin, "Her spirit is God's spirit. She is, in short, God."[59] He goes on:

> She is the wind that swept over the face of the waters at creation . . . (and) that overshadows Mary at her conception (Luke 1:35). She is the dove that descends upon Jesus at his baptism in the Jordan, and it is she who drives him into the wilderness to test his resolve . . . (She) is the Spirit who anoints him, as she anointed other prophets, to proclaim release to the captives, recovery of sight to the blind, and good news to the poor (Luke 4: 14-19). In other

words, Jesus is "the Christ," the anointed one, by virtue of having been anointed by Wisdom. In Paul's words, "Jesus is the Wisdom of God. (1 Corinthians 1:24).[60]

Jesus was a teacher of Wisdom because he was a child of Wisdom.[61] Jesus is Wisdom incarnate – the fullest manifestation of Divine Wisdom that has ever graced earth.

> # Wisdom is the Divine Presence that is the foundation of everything in existence.

Clearly, wisdom isn't simply a compendium of information or the skillful use of knowledge. Wisdom is relational. Wisdom is being aligned with the divine source of wisdom who is present in all of creation and in the hidden depths of the human soul as our truest and deepest self.

Hidden Wholeness

Wisdom is not some New Age add-on to Christianity. It is the Divine Presence that is the foundation of everything in existence. It is God's presence at work and at play in the heart of the cosmos and in the heart of each of us.

Thomas Merton's prose-poem, *Hagia Sophia,* offers a profound meditation on this Divine Presence. It begins with the following words:

> There is in all visible things an invisible fecundity, a dimmed light, a meek namelessness, a hidden wholeness. This mysterious Unity and Integrity is Wisdom, the Mother of all, *Natura naturans.*
>
> There is in all things an inexhaustible sweetness and purity, a silence that is a fount of action and joy. It rises up in wordless gentleness and flows out to me from the unseen roots of all created being, welcoming me tenderly, saluting me with indescribable humility.
>
> This is at once my own being, my own nature, and the Gift of my Creator's Thought and Art within me, speaking as Hagia Sophia, speaking as my sister, Wisdom. I am awakened; I am born again at the voice of this my Sister, sent to me from the depths of the divine fecundity.[62]

My heart soars in response to these words, even though my head cannot fully grasp what they mean.

What is this hidden wholeness, inexhaustible sweetness, and wordless gentleness that forms part of everything in existence? How does it fit with the brokenness of everything, with all of creation groaning as it awaits its redemption?[63] How can I more fully recognize this Divine Presence of Wisdom in my depths and in the world?

I cannot expect to answer these questions with my mind. But I can ponder them in my heart. And when I do I feel a surge of consoling awe and hope.

Seeing the hidden wholeness in all things is seeing God in all things. Because God is the source of everything in existence the hidden wholeness in all things is nothing less than God. This is the theological foundation for the wholeness that exists in all things. It's a theology that starts with the original blessing of God's out-flowing self and presence in everything, not with more visible brokenness with which we are all too familiar. The brokenness is very apparent and quite real. But the wholeness, although hidden, is much deeper and more fundamentally real than the brokenness because it is the God-self manifest in all things.

But how can we actually know this truth, not simply believe it? How can we increasingly see the hidden wholeness that is in all created things and hear the voice of the Silent One who speaks everywhere, particularly in the depths of our own brokenness?

We will discuss these questions much more fully in Part Two of the book but the short answer is that the route to this seeing and knowing is the alignment of our awakened minds and hearts with the mind and heart of Christ.

When the eyes of our hearts and minds are awakened we see the Divine Presence in all things. We see earth as a manifestation of God – the first incarnation of God. We see all of creation throbbing with God's presence as it becomes new and whole in Christ – everything that exists being a unique incarnation of God and expression of God's indwelling presence.

When our hearts are awakened we hear the inner voice of Wisdom and begin to recognize that this is both our own deepest nature and at the same time, the gift of God's presence within us. We recognize everything and everyone as a manifestation of God, and as our brothers and sisters. We know that everything belongs because everything is already part of the wholeness of Christ.

This is the beginning of wisdom. Everything else that is wisdom flows from this knowing.

Pausing
to Ponder

1. Take a few moments to re-read and ponder the first few sentences of Thomas Merton's poem, Hagia Sophia. What arises in your heart as you do so?

2. What do you know of the hidden wholeness that exists in everything? What do you know of it in nature? What do you know of it in yourself?

3. Trying to follow wise advice, even Biblical advice such as is found in the Book of Proverbs, is a poor substitute for hearing the voice of Wisdom in the depths of your being. Of course the two can

compliment and confirm each other but what do you know of the difference between following advice and hearing the personal voice of Wisdom? If you have never done so before, take some time to listen to the voice of Wisdom that exists in the depths of your soul and then reflect further on the relationship of wise adages and heartful attunement to the inner voice of Wisdom.

Additional Readings and Things to Ponder

For a comprehensive review of the history and theology of the Christian sapiential tradition there is no better work available than Bruno Barnhart, *The Future of Wisdom: Toward a Rebirth of Sapiential Christianity* (Rhinebeck, NY: Monkfish Publishing Company, 2018). This book is heavy going but finally now once again in print and is definitely worthy of careful attention by those who wish to dig deeper into the theological underpinnings of Christian wisdom.

The full text of Merton's poem is widely available online. One place where you can find and read it is https://thevalueofsparrows.com/2013/08/16/poetry-hagia-sophia-by-thomas-merton/

For a thoughtful theological reflection on Merton's poem I would recommend an essay by Christopher Pramuk entitled "Theodicy and the Feminine Divine: Thomas Merton's Hagia Sophia in Dialogue with Western Theology" available online at http://journals.sagepub.com/doi/pdf/10.1177/0040563915619983

For a fuller theological reflection on Christ as the wisdom of God by the same author I would recommend Christopher Pramuk' *Sophia: The Hidden Christ of Thomas Merton* (Wilmington, DE: Michael Glazier, 2009).

12 The Personal Nature of Wisdom

Discussions of wisdom almost always start with the wrong question. They start by asking, "*What* is wisdom." But, as we have just seen, they should be asking, "*Who* is Wisdom."

Starting with "What is wisdom" leads to abstractions. Any attempt to define wisdom will always be an abstraction because how could you ever hope to define a person – particularly, a Divine Person.

Hafiz says that he has a thousand brilliant lies for the question "What is God." He then goes on to explain:

> "If you think that the Truth can be known from words,
> If you think that the Sun and the Ocean
> Can pass through that tiny opening called the mouth,
> O someone should start laughing!"[64]

This is, of course, the same point that John of the Cross made when he suggested that God cannot be thought but can be loved – that is, cannot be reduced to words and known objectively at a distance, but can be known subjectively, up close and personally, in and through love.

But if God cannot be reduced to words, neither can wisdom. As you have probably noticed, this is the case for all the really important things in life – they are much harder to define than to know. Think of love, and how impossible it would be to reduce it to words, but how clearly it can be known.

Once we realize that Wisdom is a Divine person we take a step closer to seeing everything and everyone as held in Christ. And, even more importantly, we take a step closer to actually seeing through the eyes of Christ. It is the personal nature of Wisdom that gives us the possibility of the new eyes and new seeing that is so fundamental to wisdom. It is the personal nature of wisdom that allows us to become new persons.

> It's the personal nature of wisdom that allows us to become new persons.

The personal foundation of wisdom moves us out of the realm of abstractions and definitions and into the realm of relationship. It makes clear why wisdom cannot be reduced to principles, good judgment, a competency, or a way of behaving. Accessing wisdom involves acquiring the heart and mind of Christ. It simply does not get more relational or personal than that!

The Capstone Jewel

Wisdom is the capstone of both psychological and spiritual development. This is why it is a jewel of such inestimable value – and why it stands alone in being so worthy of desire.[65] It is one of the cardinal markers of maturity, wholeness, and fullness of being and alignment with the Ultimate Source of All Being.

Erik Erikson gives us a helpful framework for understanding wisdom as the capstone of psychological development.[66] Each stage of life (there are eight in his developmental framework) involves a crisis which, if successfully resolved, yields what he calls a virtue which in turn, makes a contribution to the possibility of living with wisdom. For example, the first stage (ages 0 to 1.5 years old), the crisis is related to trust versus mistrust and the virtue associated with a successful resolution of this is hope. Hope, he suggests, is the foundation for all the subsequent virtues (things such as will, purpose, competence, fidelity, love and compassion) and each adds another layer of scaffolding for the possibility of life in the mansion of wisdom.

In Erikson's view, wisdom is not accessible apart from the hard work of this entire human developmental journey. Although lots of old people never become wise, he argued that no one becomes wise unless they age well – that is, unless they successfully deal with the developmental challenges of each stage of life and by doing this, slowly build the scaffolding for wisdom to which each contributes.[67]

If wisdom is the capstone of psychological development how could it be anything less than the capstone of spiritual development? But, this is exactly what it is.

Wisdom is accessed through spiritual practices that have become woven into the fabric of daily life. Contemplative practices have a particularly important role in this process. Contemplation, or meditation, is the route to the awakening of the heart because of its unique potential to transcend the mind without abandoning it. And awakening of the heart is essential to the wisdom way of knowing.

Wisdom is deeply psychological because it arises out of the Spirit of Wisdom who is our deepest and truest self. And it is deeply spiritual because Wisdom is a personification of God. The Spirit of Wisdom is, therefore, the Spirit of God.

Wisdom always comes to us as a gift of God. Just as Solomon received his wisdom from God, so do we. There is no other way to access it and nothing we can do to achieve it.

Personal, but not Individual

Because Wisdom is personal, the wisdom journey is deeply personal. But it is also deeply relational and communal.

The Spirit of Wisdom – or if you prefer, the Spirit of God – is a face of the dance of love that Christians call the Trinity, the dance that lies at the heart of everything that is. To call it a dance of love is to recognize the Trinity as the archetype of personal, relational and communal existence. The Trinity is an exchange of love within the Divine Self that then overflows and pours out into the cosmos. This exchange and overflow of love reveals the way we access and live wisdom.

God is not a being among other beings, but the Ground of Being itself.[68] So, we might ask, what does the Trinity tell us about the nature of Being – and, therefore, of our being? It tells us that God is relationship.

And that means that we, too, are either relationship or we are nothing. Our being is, like God's, inter-being.

This is the difference between persons and individuals. To be an individual is to attempt to find your identity and meaning in yourself in isolation. To be a person is to live in a way that recognizes that your unique identity and meaning will always be found in relationships. Personhood is dynamic and relational, never static or individual. It is inter-being, not independence.

> Wisdom is not an individual achievement. It is always accessed and lived in relationships and communities.

Wisdom is not an individual achievement. At best, all an individual can do is minimize foolishness – and even that is a tall order. Wisdom is personal because the Spirit of Wisdom is the Spirit of God. The Spirit of Wisdom is forever a part of the community that is the Godhead that flows outward in loving self-expression into the rest of the cosmos. Wisdom, therefore, will always be accessed and lived in relationships and communities.

We must walk the wisdom path with others who long for the awakening and transformation that we long for, and we must be prepared to learn and grow together with them. Walking this path we discover that personal well-being cannot be achieved apart from the well-being of the larger spheres in which we find our belonging – our families, our communities, our nations, our world and our universe. As we learn to see all of life through God's eyes, slowly but surely our center of gravity shifts from our mind to our heart, and our consciousness and identity expand. Slowly but surely we move from duality to integrality as we increasingly relate to life not by differentiation and judgment but with compassion for all that share earth as our home. Slowly but surely we are transformed and we become more whole.

Participating in the Dance

This is the transformational path that Jesus walked and lived. At the core of this path is dying to the egoic self and coming to newness of life in the truth of our self-in-Christ. This is how we not only access the mind of Christ but allow it to flow through us. This is the way in which we participate in the dance that is the life of the Trinity.

Carl McColman describes this participation in the dance of the Trinity as follows:

> God is in us because we are in Christ. As members of the mystical body, Christians partake in the divine nature of the Trinity. We do not merely watch the dance, we dance the dance. We join hands with Christ and the Spirit flows through us and between us and our feet move always in the loving embrace of the Father. In that we are members of the mystical body of Christ, we see the joyful love of the Father through the eyes of the Son. And with every breath, we breathe the Holy Spirit.[69]

Knowing that God is in us, just as we are in Christ, is the result of awakenings that open the eyes of our heart and allow us to see through the eyes, mind and heart of Christ. It is these new eyes of Wisdom that allow us to live with deep awareness of the sacredness and interconnectedness of everything in existence.

Like the astronauts who went to the moon but came back most impacted by seeing earth from a new perspective, we no longer see an earth divided by national, ethnic, geographic or religious boundaries but a single living planet that we all share as our home. From this awakened perspective we recognize how essential it is that we not hide behind or fear differences but learn to honor, cherish and nurture the diversity of life in all its forms – human and non-human.

This is the wisdom that begins to flow from the recognition that we are all one in Christ – one body, one people, and one global community aboard the same fragile and increasingly vulnerable spaceship that we call earth. Caring for that earth and all its inhabitants becomes an obvious priority. Social justice and eco-spirituality are easily recognized as essential parts of simply being responsible humans. We no longer need to be convinced of the importance of taking care of our bodies or our inner selves. All these things are quickly recognized as part of living wisdom.

Seeing through these new eyes of Wisdom allows us to see the real, not just the apparent. It allows us, therefore, to see God in everyone and everything. It makes it possible for us to live in alignment with the creative Spirit of Wisdom who inhabits all of creation and who is our truest and deepest self.

Seeing through the new eyes of Wisdom we discover that personal well-being cannot be achieved apart from the well-being of the larger spheres in which we find our belonging – our families, our communities, our nations, our world and our universe. And, as we learn to see all of life through God's eyes, slowly but surely our center of gravity shifts from our minds to our hearts, and our consciousness and identity expand. Slowly but surely we become more whole and we become wise.

This is the wisdom I seek, and, having gotten this far in the book, I suspect it is the wisdom you also seek. Like me, I suspect that you also seek to access it, not merely understand it.

That is what we now turn to – the question of how we walk the path of wisdom so that we might eventually fully inhabit the mind and heart of Christ.

Pausing
to Ponder

1. Think for a moment about the difference between Wisdom as an impersonal body of knowledge and Wisdom as a Divine Person. What implications might this hold for your personal wisdom quest?

2. Reflect further on the difference I suggested between individuals and persons. To what extent do you find your identity and

meaning in yourself as an individual? What do you know of your identity and meaning that is based on relationships, on being part of a larger whole? What difference do you sense between being an individual versus being a person?

Additional Readings and Things to Ponder

For an excellent overview of the Christian wisdom tradition and how we have lost this part of our heritage I recommend Bruno Barnhart, *The Future of Wisdom: Toward a Rebirth of Sapiential Christianity*, (Rhinebeck, NY: Monkfish Book Publishing Company, 2018).

As a follow-up to the discussion of the Trinity, I also recommend Richard Rohr, *The Divine Dance: The Trinity and Your Transformation* (New Kensington, PA: Whitaker House, 2016).

Part Two   Accessing Wisdom

In Part Two we move into the heart of our topic as we consider the question of how we can access this jewel of inestimable value. Deepening our access to wisdom involves desire, awakening, faith, and transformation. Through their interplay we receive the gifts of expanded consciousness and identity. The traditional Christian name for this new consciousness is the mind of Christ, and for our new identity, being in Christ.

"Let this same mind be in you
that was in Christ Jesus."
Philippians 2:5[70]

13 Desire

It is hard to overestimate the power and influence of our desires on the human journey. More often than we realize, we get what we desire and do not get things we do not desire.

Of course, we also get things we would never choose and no amount of desire can protect us from these unwelcome experiences. But this does not diminish the power of desire.

Thomas Merton describes the influence of our desires in even stronger terms: "Life is shaped by the end you live for. You are made in the image of what you desire."[71]

Desires shape not simply what we get but much more importantly, who and what we become. They shape our very being. As I have said elsewhere:

> A desire for wealth leads to greed, envy and dissatisfaction. A desire for power saps compassion, just as a desire for reputation feeds self-preoccupation. And a desire for respect leads to an overinvestment in image.[72]

As strong an influence as desires are on the human journey, they are even more powerful and important in our spiritual journey. The spiritual journey is fueled by desire. No desire equals no spiritual unfolding.

Will is simply never up to the task of pushing us forward in our spiritual journey. In contrast, however, our deepest desires pull us forward as our longing shapes a posture of leaning into that for which our hearts most deeply ache.[73]

What do You Want?

The Gospels describe an interesting conversation between Jesus, James and John that cuts to the heart of this question of desires. Jesus asked them what they want from him.[74] It isn't an easy question to answer. But, it is a good one.

I recall a spiritual director I was hoping to work with once asking me the same question. As part of an initial phone conversation she asked me to take as long as I needed, but not less than a month, to reflect on what I wanted from her and what I wanted from God – and then call back to arrange a first appointment. The wisdom of this advice only became clear after I spent 6 weeks reflecting on her question and finally felt I knew what I most deeply desired.

> By those who love wisdom, she is readily seen; by those who seek her, she is readily found.

Wisdom wasn't at the top of my list at that point. In fact, it wasn't even on the list. It took a while before I realized how important it was and before I began to seriously desire it. This is part of the aging well that prepares us to seriously begin to seek wisdom.

Recall the words of the Book of Wisdom that speak of how Wisdom is found:

> By those who love wisdom, she is readily seen; by those who seek her, she is readily found. She anticipates those who desire her by making herself known first. Whoever gets up early to seek her will have no trouble but will find her sitting at the door for she herself searches everywhere for those who are worthy of her, benevolently appearing to them on their ways, anticipating their every thought.[75]

Wisdom will only be found by those who desire and seek her. This brings us back to the question of what you desire.

Desire for wisdom emerges out of life experience. No one is born with it and seldom do people possess both sufficient maturity and rich enough life experience to even think about wisdom until they reach their thirties or forties. Some may consider it a potentially useful competency but this is not the same as desire.

The jewel of inestimable value must be desired for who she is if Wisdom is to be acquired. But as our longings become focused through life we become better able to recognize more specific dimensions of our desire. This is the soil out of which a longing for Wisdom will usually emerge.

Preparing for the Wisdom Journey

Marcel Proust tells us that no one can give us wisdom; we must discover it for ourselves. He then goes on to say that finding it involves "a journey through the wilderness which no one else can take for us, and effort which no one can spare us."[76]

There are no shortcuts to acquiring wisdom. And Proust is correct. The journey is more like a trek through the wilderness than a walk in a park. Wisdom arises out of life lived well, not simply from reading or listening to those who are wiser, and certainly not from understanding the theory or theology of wisdom acquisition.

So what is this wisdom journey?

- It is the journey of life lived soulfully and intentionally – this including such things as living with presence, wonder, surrender, gratitude, and a relentless embrace of reality.[77]

- It is living our life within the context of spiritual practices that have been woven into the fabric of daily life, especially contemplative or meditative practices (because of the crucial role they play in the awakening of the heart).[78]

- It is journeying with others as we realize that personal well-being cannot be achieved apart from the well-being of the larger spheres in which we find our belonging – our families, our communities, our nations, our world and our universe.[79]

Lived long enough, life will always give us enough experience with foolishness that we begin to see just how important wisdom truly is. Sadly, it takes quite a while for most of us to come to the point of learning that lesson from our mistakes. There is, however, no alternate route to wisdom apart from this discovery and our own deep longing for it.

Longing for wisdom emerges from an honest and full-hearted embrace of our mistakes and foolishness – no matter how hard this is. Apart from this, we will forever be blinded by our arrogance and narcissism and unable to truly become wise.

Your wisdom journey has begun when you are able to recognize that everything in your life belongs.

You will only be truly ready to embark on the wisdom journey when you can see everything in your life as preparation for the present moment. But you must be ready to accept absolutely everything, eliminating none of it.

Proust suggests that the wisdom we see and admire in others is not the result of good education or parenting but has developed out of the soil of a total life experience.[80] Even the things we would never have chosen to be part of our story are the things that carry with them the most precious gifts for our becoming whole and wise.

Your wisdom journey has begun when you are able to recognize that everything in your life belongs. Everything you have done and everything that was ever done to you has been crucial preparation to the next steps you are now ready to take. And, looking at your life, from a place that may surprise you, you are able to say, "It is what it is" and "Even the 'bad' was good."[81]

This is the soil out of which true desire for wisdom emerges. This is the graced place that lets you know that you are now ready for awakening.

Pausing

to Ponder

---

1. *Think for a moment about Thomas Merton's assertion that life is shaped by the end you live for, and that you are made in the image of what you desire. Looking back over your life, what desires have shaped who you have become?*

2. *What do you most deeply long for at this point in your life? Take some time to answer this question as you follow more superficial desires to their deeper sources and begin to discern the contours of your deepest desires.*

3. *In this chapter I suggested three things that form an essential part of a wisdom journey: 1) living soulfully and intentionally, 2) within the context of spiritual practices that have been woven into the fabric of our lives, and 3) journeying with others. To what extent do these things characterize your journey at this point? What invitations do you hear for yourself as you reflect on this?*

Additional Readings and Things to Ponder

For more on coming to know your deepest desires, I recommend Margaret Silf, *Inner Compass: An Invitation to Ignatian Spirituality* (Chicago, IL: Loyola Press, 2007). This book is a wonderful introduction to the wisdom of St. Ignatius related to discernment. Truly knowing our deepest desires is the foundation of discerning our motivations and cultivating wisdom and this book is, in my opinion, unequalled in the help it provides in this process.

1. to serve + glorify God. to love. to share "truth" BUT also, to be well thought of, influential, admired

2. to be one w/ Christ. to abide in love. to be a safe, wise guy priest.

3. 1) somewhat, 2) yes, 3) not so much

14 Awakening

As powerful as desires are, they are not strong enough to pull us out of our inner preoccupations. In fact, they usually contribute to our mindless oblivion.

Most of us go through life as sleep walkers. We are born asleep, we marry and breed children in our sleep, we work asleep, and we die in our sleep – never having awakened and never realizing that we missed knowing the preciousness of our life. We may rise out of our slumber for brief moments of intense emotional experience but we quickly slip back into a somnambulistic fog. This fog is the tangled web of our thoughts, fantasies, memories, plans, and desires – all the things that keep us preoccupied with ourselves and block us from being truly present to the present moment.

When we are caught up in this fog we live as robots. We do all the things others do around us but almost all of them are also simply living their lives on auto-pilot. They are no more truly awake and truly present than us.

We will never find Wisdom while we are on auto-pilot. The place where she waits to meet us is a place the auto-pilot is programmed to avoid. Wisdom doesn't wait for us in the temple, academy or library where we might expect to find her. She waits for us in the midst of the flow of ordinary life. She appears to us in the streets of the city as we are making our way through the mundane details of our lives.[82]

Wisdom is present and patiently waiting for us. But if we are to notice her we must also be present. That is what awakening is all about. It is a call into presence that is sufficiently strong and clear that we don't immediately fall back again into sleep.

Wisdom's Alarm Clocks

Most people prefer falling asleep to awakening. We resist waking by shutting off the alarm, pulling the pillow over our heads, and falling back asleep – sometimes shutting it off so fast that it hardly disturbs our sleep!

Spiritual awakening is much the same. Although the spiritual alarm clocks are different for each of us, we respond to their wake-up calls with the same annoyance and resistance and very quickly return to our slumbering auto-pilot mode of existence.

Wisdom masters offer help to people who want to awaken. The wise ones don't try to awaken others but offer gentle disruptions to their sleep that function as an invitation to awakening.

A favorite of these gentle alarms used by wisdom masters in the East has always been pithy but provocative stories. The Gospels describe the stories Jesus used as parables and they certainly fit this description of pithy and provocative. If they no longer sound disturbing to us it is simply because we have become too familiar with them.

Heard with fresh ears, the stories of Jesus are as troubling as a Zen koan. Their purpose is to cause sufficient inner disruption that hearers will be jarred into sufficient reflective openness of heart and mind that may notice the invitation to awakening.

Put yourself in the shoes of Nicodemus as you listen his conversation Jesus and sense the inner disruption it must have produced. Approaching Jesus by night out of fear of being seen by his fellow-Pharisees, Nicodemus initiates the conversation by asking Jesus the following question:

> "Rabbi, we know that you are a teacher come from God, for no one can do these signs that you do unless God is with him."
>
> Jesus answered him, "Truly, truly, I say to you, unless one is born again he cannot see the kingdom of God."
>
> Nicodemus said to him, "How can a man be born when he is old? Can he enter a second time into his mother's womb and be born?
>
> Jesus answered, "Truly, truly I say to you, unless one is born of water and the Spirit, he cannot enter the kingdom of God."[83]

This would have made no more sense to Nicodemus than if a Japanese Zen master asked him to ponder the sound of one hand clapping. But it served the same purpose. Like any good wisdom alarm it offered enough provocation and inner disruption that Nicodemus was forced to realize that this notion of being born again could never be understood by the mind. And this is the way an invitation to awaken works. It invites attention, pause, reflection, and an opening of mind and heart space.

The same is true of all the crazy wisdom taught by Jesus that we noticed in Chapter Two – things like, to find your life you must first lose it, to achieve eternal treasures you must abandon all your earthly possession, and, to become truly free you must allow yourself to be enslaved.

> Spiritual practices do not produce awakening. But they increase the chances that you won't be asleep when the invitations to awaken come.

Anthony de Mello was the twentieth century Christian mystic who has probably done more than anyone else to bring together the spiritual wisdom of East and West. An Indian Jesuit priest from Bombay, the almost exclusive focus of his teaching was the importance of awakening. Like Jesus, he told stories designed, in his words, "not to instruct, but to awaken." Most of his stories involve the baffling sayings of a Master in conversation with his disciples. Here is one of them about awakening, something he often referred to as enlightenment.

"What does one need to be enlightened?" asked the disciples. Said the Master, "You must discover what it is that falls in the water and does not make a ripple; moves through the trees and does not make a sound; enters a field and does not stir a single blade of grass."

After weeks of fruitless pondering, the disciples said, "What is this thing?"

"Thing," said the Master. "But it isn't a thing at all."

"So it's nothing?"

"You might say so."

"Then how do we search for it?"

"Did I tell you to search for it? It can be found, but never searched for. Seek and you will miss."[84]

De Mello's point is that nothing you do will produce awakening. You can desire it, but don't waste your time trying to produce it. Trying to awaken yourself is simply a distraction that helps you defend against true awakening.

He follows this up in another conversation between a disciple and a Master:

"Is there anything I can do to make myself enlightened?"
"As little as you can do to make the sun rise in the morning."
"Then of what use are the spiritual exercises you prescribe?"
"To make sure you are not asleep when the sun begins to rise."[85]

Spiritual practices are preparation for receiving God's gifts. They do not produce awakening. Sadly, it all too possible for Christians to believe the right things (orthodoxy) and even do the right things (orthopraxy) but never experience the awakenings that consent initiates. But while spiritual practices do not produce awakening they do increase the chances that you won't be asleep when the invitations to awaken come.

Awakening is the foundational spiritual grace. Without it, there can be no transformation and without transformation, there can be no genuine wisdom acquisition.

Welcoming Awareness

Sleep is comfortable. It allows us to hide in the tangled web of our neurotic fantasies and avoid the harsh light that would expose our illusions and deceits. Waking, in contrast, is uncomfortable. Reality is often unpleasant and our defenses against it, ugly. So our default response is to avoid waking at all costs.

Waking starts with awareness. But, normally that first shimmering ray of awareness is not strong enough to fully awaken us. It's more like a daydream; we are dimly aware of a gentle invitation to awaken but are still asleep and enjoying it. However, the awareness that threatens to disturb our sleep does hold enough potential that when we respond with a desire to awaken and offer our consent, waking can occur.

Invitations to awaken are generally more like a nudge than fireworks – although dramatic awakenings, such as experienced by Saul on the road to Damascus, still occur. Invitations can come in many forms. Generally they emerge from the circumstances of our life. A divorce, financial or medical crisis, a death of a loved one or any other major loss or failure can all contain an invitation to awaken. Even aging can do the same. But consent to awakening is quite different from our default posture of trying to get back to how things were before the disruption. Consent generally only arises when the internal conflict and disruption of meaning and self-coherence is so strong that we realize that our way of being has to change.

Desire to awaken and consent to its transformational potential (which we always sense, at least unconsciously) emerge out of the space that invitations to awaken present to our minds and hearts. That's what inner disruptions do. They give us pause. And waking only happens when we embrace that pause and offer our consent to the awakening that is emerging within us.

Glimpses in the Fog

As the light of awareness begins to grow one of the first things you may recognize is that you are not who you think you are. At the core of the fog of spiritual sleep is the crazy web of lies we build around who we think we are. You might, for example, have thought that you are a success (or a failure), mature (or hopelessly immature), intelligent (or dumb) or any number of other things. But none of these things are qualities of existence. They are simply labels. They are no more you than your feelings are you. You are not reducible to any of them.

This is where the spiritual practice of meditation or contemplative prayer enters the picture. Nothing is as powerful a way of helping us cut through the tangled web of mis-identifications as these contemplative practices because of the way in which they help us dis-identify with our thoughts, emotions and other things that arise in consciousness when we are still.

You are not your depression or anxiety. Those things are just feelings. Similarly, you are not your profession, your history, your accomplishments, your roles or your reputation. But it takes a genuine awakening to help us begin to dis-identify with the lies that entangle our essential self and keep us from knowing our fundamental freedom and lightness of being.

St. Teresa of Avila said that God gave her the grace of dis-identifying herself from herself.[86] What she meant was that she recognized the things she had previously understood to be herself as lies and was now free of them. If she was living now she might speak of it terms of recognizing and releasing her false self and embracing the truth of her self-in-Christ – all of this being something she received as a gift of God.

This is often the first fruit of awakening. It emerges out of the dawning awareness of the reality of our divine likeness. It is the seed that, with grace and nurture, will take root and eventually bloom into our transformed identity and consciousness. It is a refusal to be defined by anything that reduces or limits our divine likeness and kinship. And it is always accompanied by a new-found sense of freedom.

Freedom

Anthony de Mello tells us that one of the best markers of awakening is freedom, just as suffering is one of the best markers of sleep. All suffering is caused by our identifying our self with something, whether that something is inside or outside us. And all freedom is, at core, freedom from those mis-identifications.

The freedom we begin to experience in awakening is the freedom of walking out of Plato's cave[87] and, for the first time, seeing reality, not merely the illusions that had been accepted as reality.

De Mello describes this freedom by means of a story about an Irish prisoner who dug a tunnel under the prison wall and managed to escape. He came out right in the middle of a school playground where little children were running about, jumping and playing games. Finally emerging into the light he couldn't restrain himself and he began to jump up and down, crying, "I'm free, I'm free, I'm free!" A little girl in the playground looked at him scornfully and said, "That's nothing. I'm four."[88]

Freedom does not lie in external circumstances. It resides in the heart. It resides in the heart because authentic awakening always involves the heart. Sometimes the awakening will start in the mind and move to the heart and sometimes it will start in the heart and move to the mind.[89] However, because most of us live more in the mind than the heart, it is crucial that the heart be awakened and the mind assimilated within this deeper center of our being.

Once your mind and heart have been awakened no one can enslave you. In fact, like the escaped prisoner in the school yard, you will smile at any mocking or misunderstanding you encounter because you have released your need to be treated in a precious way. You now know the preciousness of life and the freedom of being awake.

Pausing

to Ponder

---

1. *What things make you reluctant or unable to embrace wakefulness more fully? What do you get out of avoiding it?* fear, facing myself

2. *What invitations to awaken have you experienced in the last few years but avoided? To what invitations to awaken have you offered your consent?* both? John's death + Dad's, Ben's "spiritual" journey

3. *I suggested in this chapter that awakening is more like a crisis than an accomplishment. It involves inner disruption. How did you respond? How would faith and your inner promptings have led you to respond?*

4. *What mis-identifications can you notice in yourself? How might they contribute to your suffering and keep you from freedom? What do you know of the freedom that comes from releasing mis-identifications?* judging — or living in that realm (fearing judging too) needing affirmation / approval

Additional Readings and Things to Ponder

A great follow-up to this chapter is Anthony de Mello, *Awakening: Conversations with the Masters* (New York: NY: Image, 2003). Settle in for some gentle humor but deep teaching as the master storyteller shares with you some of his teaching stories about awakening.

Another helpful discussion of awakening is Anthony de Mello, *Awareness* (New York: NY: Image, 1992). This book is available as a free PDF at www.arvindguptatoys.com/arvindgupta/tonyawareness.pdf
A free audio version of this book is available online at
https://www.youtube.com/watch?v=qydwdAusCW8&feature=youtu.be

15 Faith

The meaning of awakenings is always developed within the context of our faith. How we understand an experience of awakening and how we respond to it both require the context of our spiritual tradition. Faith therefore plays an indispensible role in wisdom acquisition.

But, before I say more about what I mean by faith perhaps now is a good time to clarify what I mean by two other terms I have introduced, and say something about how they relate to each other.

Awakening is the foundation of everything else in spiritual unfolding and wisdom acquisition. As I said at the close of the last chapter, awakening involves both the heart and the mind as both are essential in accessing wisdom. However, awakening is more of a means than an end. The end is transformation.

Transformation is the term I use to describe what others sometime call enlightenment. It refers to the quantum shifts in the organization of self that involve at least two things – an enduring expansion of consciousness and a broader, more inclusive identity. We experience the expansion of consciousness as increased awareness of the interconnectedness of everything in existence. And we experience the expansion of identity as deep personal knowing of the truth of our self in Christ, Christ in us, and others – others being now seen as our siblings in Christ, both we and they parts of the same larger whole.

Transformation involves awakening but, in my experience, it never occurs with single awakening. First awakenings are limited and partial.

But when received with faith and consent, they build upon themselves, slowly becoming a cascading series of moments of enlightenment that gain traction in pulling us toward the point of no return. That point is the tipping point I refer to as transformation.[90]

These quantum shifts will be our focus in the next two chapters but now let me return to the question of faith. Barnhart suggests that faith is the fundamental form of Christian wisdom knowing.[91] Because this is my own path and because I suspect Christians will be the primary readers of this book, let me say more about what I mean by the term and the role it plays in awakening, transformation, and accessing wisdom.

Beliefs and Trust

When I suggest that the meaning and significance of awakenings are always developed within the context of our faith I am using the term "faith" in two ways – faith as beliefs and faith as trust.

Our beliefs will always shape our understanding of an awakening. And often they will be changed by it. Sometimes the changes will be dramatic (as in the conversion of St. Paul) and sometimes they will be modest. But they will form part of the picture as we seek to make sense of each experience of inner awakening.

However, any experience that remains at the level of changed beliefs is not worthy of being called an awakening because it has not moved beyond the mind. Beliefs are a product of the mind. They are our way of making sense of something. The more important we think the understanding to be, the more strongly we tend to embrace the belief.

But it always remains simply a construal – that is, a thought or an understanding.

This is why I have said that authentic awakenings that start in the mind will always also involve the heart. New ways of seeing emerge from the heart, not just the mind. The best the mind can produce is beliefs and beliefs – even new beliefs – are not sufficient to access wisdom.

> When faith is reduced to beliefs it is our beliefs in which we trust.

Wisdom emerges from a changed consciousness, not merely changed beliefs. It is associated with new ways of knowing, not merely new knowledge. It requires a new heart and a renewed mind.

This brings us to the second and much more important way in which I am using the term "faith" when I say that faith forms an integral part of this wisdom journey – namely, faith as trust.

Trust is the core of faith. Christian faith is trust in God. Think of Abraham. The New Testament describes him as a champion of faith. Abraham didn't demonstrate that faith by believing certain propositions about God but by demonstrating enough trust to leave his home in one of the greatest cities of the ancient world and head into the wilderness to a place God said he would be shown as he travelled. This is trust in action. This is what counts on the Christian path. And it is this trust that is so essential in walking the Christian wisdom path.

When faith is reduced to beliefs it is our beliefs in which we trust. Even if they are beliefs about God this is not the same as trust in God. Think of the confidence fundamentalists place in their beliefs. They have absolute certainty that their beliefs are perfect representations of ultimate reality. And so they clutch these beliefs close to their chest, protect them as their most treasured possession, and worship them as if they were God.

Certainty in life is never possible. Those who seek that certainty through religious beliefs that they take to be absolute truths and then build their lives around the shrine of their beliefs delude themselves. If certainty were possible we would not need faith! But life cannot be lived without faith – not faith as beliefs but faith as trust.

Beliefs should not be what we look *at* but what we look *through*. Our beliefs – particularly our religious beliefs, should provide illumination that helps us see.

Simone Weil compared religious beliefs or doctrine to a flashlight. When we look at the bulb we get no illumination. Instead, it blinds us. But when we use it to cast light in the dark places of the world or our selves, it allows us to see what truly is. This is what it means to see through the eyes of faith.[92]

Beliefs point us toward ultimate reality. However, as Anthony de Mello reminds us, our words, thoughts and beliefs about God are simply fingers pointing *toward* God. Sadly, too often we confuse God with our finger and remain content to look at it instead of God!

Beliefs and the Roadmap

Beliefs form the framework of our theology and good theology provides us with a potentially helpful roadmap for the wisdom journey. However, if wisdom does not even appear on the radar of your present theological framework then your theology will provide you with little on the wisdom journey.

Any adequate theological wisdom roadmap will have to provide those of us following the Christian transformational path with a number of things, but let me just focus on only one. If you are to access the mind of Christ you will need to know about Jesus of Nazareth (which most Christians do), but also you will need to know about Christ (which most Christians do not). And you will also need to know how Jesus and Christ are related.

Most Christians know that Christ is a title given to Jesus by the early Christians. It means "the anointed one." However, because this title has become so familiar, many Christians speak of Jesus and Christ interchangeably – often in a way that suggests that Christ is the last name of Jesus. This shows a serious misunderstanding that has significant implications for acquiring wisdom – which in Scriptures, is described as putting on the mind of Christ[93], never as putting on the mind of Jesus.

With few exceptions over the last 2000 years, Christianity has focused more on Jesus than Christ. The resulting religion might be better described as Jesusanity than Christianity. When we only focus on the historic Jesus and treat Christ merely as a title we lose sight of the bigger story of the cosmic Christ that gives Jesus his real significance.

"God has made him both Lord and Christ, this Jesus whom you crucified."

Christ means Messiah, not some "cosmic" NO

On the day of Pentecost, after acknowledging the eternal presence of the Holy Spirit, Peter proclaimed that Jesus reveals the Christ.[94] This brings together the personal and historic with the cosmic and universal.[95] Jesus is the microcosm that reveals the truth of the macrocosm. In the words of Richard Rohr, "In Jesus the Timeless Christ became time bound."[96] In Jesus we encounter the possibility of coming to know and love both the eternal Christ and the first century Jesus of Nazareth.

NO ?

According to Scriptures, "Christ is the radiant light of God's glory and the perfect copy of God's nature, sustaining the universe by God's powerful command."[97] But notice, this is Christ, not Jesus. It was this Cosmic and Risen Christ who appeared to Saul on the road to Damascus, not Jesus. Like us, Paul never met Jesus directly and hardly ever quotes him. It was Christ who was the constant focus of his preaching and writing – the Christ who Jesus revealed through his life, death and especially, through his resurrection.

maybe "his Son"

> Jesus is the union of human and divine within time; Christ is the eternal union of matter and spirit.

In the words of Richard Rohr, "The resurrection of Jesus was the symbolic way of saying his presence was beyond any limits of physical space and time. Jesus was historically bound; the Christ is

May be heretical?

omnipresent."[98] Although this understanding of the relationship of Jesus and Christ might be unfamiliar, it shouldn't be. The presence of the Cosmic Christ is inescapable in such places in Scriptures as Colossians 1, Ephesians 1, John 1, I John 1, and Hebrews 1. This was the starting point of the authors of these books. How could we have missed their message? How could we have missed the fact that "Jesus is the union of human and divine in one person, and the Christ is the eternal union of matter and Spirit from the beginning of time."[99]

The bottom line is that we need both Jesus and Christ. "Jesus without Christ invariably becomes a time-bound and culturally-bound religion that excludes much of humanity from Christ's embrace. On the other end, Christ without Jesus would easily become an abstract metaphysics or a mere ideology without personal engagement. We must believe in Jesus *and* Christ."[100]

Trust and the Transformational Journey

But while faith-as-beliefs has an important role to play in walking the wisdom path, faith-as-trust is absolutely crucial if we are to experience the transformation of our mind and heart into the mind and heart of Christ.

Trust in God is essential at every step on the transformational journey of sapiential Christianity. It's a journey that invites us, like Abraham, to leave the comfortable and familiar places where we are without any precise promise of where we are being asked to go or what the journey will involve.

We have already seen how this begins with awakenings. Each awakening offers us an invitation to leave the tangled web of our thoughts, fantasies, memories, plans, and desires and trust the glimpses of a larger and truer reality that we sense in moments of spiritual emergence. I described the place from which we are invited to awaken as the fog. Awakenings give us a momentary and partial lifting of the fog as they provide us with a hint of the larger realities that hold us.

Nothing is as disorienting as thick fog when you are in the midst of it. I say that as someone who has spent a lot of time sailing in fog – literally, not metaphorically. And, as any sailor will tell you, there is absolutely nothing that will more quickly and profoundly make you doubt your compass (and any other directional and positional instruments you may have on board) than being in the midst of fog that is so thick that you can't see even the bow of your boat. It is as if the fog that is all around you suddenly has found a way to engulf your brain.

Because dense fog also intensifies sounds it amplifies the disorientation that quickly sets in. It makes you want to drop all sails and simply sit absolutely still until the fog lifts. But usually this is neither possible nor wise.

It takes great faith to sail in these conditions. And it takes great trust in God to keep moving forward toward awakening in conditions of spiritual fog. You feel profoundly disoriented and confused – unsure if you are going forward or backward, unsure if you are right side up or upside down.

Listen to Thomas Merton express his trust in God in the midst of a devastating period of spiritual fog:

> My Lord God,
> I have no idea where I am going.
> I do not see the road ahead of me.
> I cannot know for certain
> where it will end.
>
> Nor do I really know myself,
> and that I think I am following your will
> does not mean I am actually doing so.
>
> But I believe
> the desire to please you
> does in fact please you.
> And I hope I have that desire
> in all I am doing.
>
> I hope I will never do anything
> apart from that desire.
> And I know if I do this
> you will lead me by the right road
> though I may know nothing about it.
>
> I will trust you always
> though I may seem to be lost
> and in the shadow of death.

I will not fear,

for you will never leave me

to face my perils alone.[101]

It is terrifying to feel that disoriented, that profoundly uncertain, that incapable of trusting your own mind, senses and perception. I know. I have been there. Without faith we would be crushed by those moments. Faith in God is trusting that, despite all feelings and appearances, God is with us, inviting us to continue to walk forward, step by step, in the darkness. It is trusting God enough to allow ourselves to fall into the dark river that is God and go with the flow without seeing. It is trusting God sufficiently that we can enter the Cloud of Unknowing.[102]

It also takes great trust in God to trust what we sense in these moments of awakening. Was that really a glimpse of reality, or was it an illusion? Was that really of God, or was it a product of our imagination?

> Faith-as-trust helps us calibrate and trust the eyes of our awakening heart.

And it takes trust in God to trust the hope that begins to arise in the darkness of spiritual fog. There is nothing more dangerous than false hope. But faith grounds hope and allows it to serve as the beacon we need as we move ahead in the fog.

Faith-as-trust allows us to resist the temptation to ignore the awakening and go back to sleep. Seen through the eyes of our faith, we are able to discern God's presence in the midst of the fog, calling us forward, and accompanying us as we do so.

Over time, seeing through the eyes of our faith-as-trust helps us calibrate and trust the eyes of our awakening heart. Without this we can never come to know the Spirit of Wisdom who is our deepest and truest self. Without this we will forever be looking for Wisdom somewhere outside of and beyond us. Trust in God becomes the basis of trust in our own awakening hearts, and in the Spirit of Wisdom who resides there.

Transformation always feels more like a crisis than an accomplishment. It occurs in the midst of inner disruption that feels like we are left with no alternative to releasing old frameworks of understanding and living before we have a good sense of what will replace them. It involves stepping off one platform before having a foot on another. Transformation is more like a leap of faith than a small step of a safe, controlled journey. This is why faith is so central to walking the wisdom path. It prepares us for the free-fall that is always a part of transformation.

It takes trust in God to even ask for Wisdom – not simply knowledge or understanding, but the guiding presence of Spirit of Wisdom as our inner compass. It takes trust in God to fully lean into the wisdom of God as our moment-by-moment gold-standard reference point for life. It takes trust in God to choose the eyes of Christ for seeing and judging actions and making sense of life. It takes trust in God to choose the mind and heart of Christ for processing experiencing and discerning truth.

But none of this should surprise us since the wisdom path lies right at the core of Christian spirituality. And it's hard to imagine how any spiritual path that does not place faith at its core could ever be considered Christian!

Pausing to Ponder

the way David describes it

1. *How do you understand faith? Given that understanding, what is the role of faith within the spiritual journey?*

I think "Jesus" appears in Acts..

2. *How do you understand the relationship between Jesus and Christ? How do you respond to the understanding presented in this chapter of Jesus as historic (time-bound) and Christ as eternal and omnipresent – or, Jesus as the union of human and divine and Christ as the eternal union of matter and Spirit?*

3. *How helpful has your faith been in the midst of profound periods of spiritual fog? What do you know about trusting God in the darkness when you cannot see your way ahead?*

very helpful –

Additional Readings and Things to Ponder

For a short but helpful discussion of the Biblical foundation for understanding faith as trust, see John Schoenheit's blog, *Faith is Trust* - http://thesowermagazine.com/faith-is-trust/

For more on the contribution of Simone Weil to an understanding of Christian faith as illumination, listen to the three-part audio podcast by David Cayley called *Enlightened by Love: The Thought of Simone Weil*: http://www.davidcayley.com/podcasts/2014/11/30/1msu5jd829w2gqhjxrs kf3blbmsp0y or read a transcript of these podcasts at https://static1.squarespace.com/static/542c2af8e4b00b7cfca08972/t/58ff 834a5016e158263f7e09/1493140304361/Enlightened+by+Love.pdf

16   Transformation: Christian Theological Foundations

The starting point for understanding transformation from a Christian point of view is the Bible's rich images, metaphors and teachings about conversion.

We have already encountered the metaphor of being born again. It reminds us that transformation is a work of the Spirit of God. But let me start with by far the most frequently occurring New Testament metaphor, one that I think is more helpful in understanding wisdom acquisition – the Kingdom of Heaven. We will then also look at the closely related teaching of making the mind of Christ our own.

The Kingdom of Heaven

The Kingdom of Heaven (sometimes referred to as the Kingdom of God) was a constant theme in the teaching of Jesus – the phrase appearing in the Gospels more than one hundred times. Jesus obviously thought the Kingdom was very important. So, *what* is it and *why* is it so important?

Many Christians assume that the Kingdom of Heaven refers to the place where they expect to go when they die. But the problem with this interpretation is that Jesus himself specifically contradicts it when he says, The Kingdom of Heaven is *within* you[103](that is, here) and *at hand*[104] (that is, now). Cynthia Bourgeault suggests, "*You don't die into it; you awaken into it.*"[105]

Another misinterpretation of the Kingdom of Heaven is to view it as an earthly utopia – a realm of peace and justice. But Jesus also rejected this with his unambiguous assertion that, "My kingdom is not of this world."[106]

Jim Marion, a twenty first century American mystic, offers what I find to be a very helpful understanding of the Kingdom of Heaven suggesting that it isn't a place but a state. More specifically, it is a state of consciousness.[107] This helps us understand the inner dimension of the Kingdom of Heaven but also the fact that it is both here and now *and* yet to find its fullness in the future.

While we access the Kingdom of Heaven by going within ourselves, that which begins internally subsequently reveals itself externally. Consciousness is private but a transformed consciousness cannot exist without breaking through those bounds of privacy and spilling out into the world. That is the nature of transformation – and the nature of the Kingdom of Heaven.

> Kingdom consciousness is seeing through the mind and heart of Christ.

For Jesus, the Kingdom state of consciousness was something that could be realized by everyone, right now, here on earth. It can be seen with the eyes of the heart. The goal of the whole spiritual life according to Jesus was to seek and enter this Kingdom consciousness, for once we have entered it, everything else will be added.[108]

Kingdom consciousness is seeing through the mind and heart of Christ. This means that we see what Jesus saw and know what Jesus knew. So, what exactly did Jesus see, and what is it that we will see once we see through Kingdom eyes? As Scriptures reveal, we will see God since Jesus saw God in everything and everyone.

James Finley elaborates:

> What's fascinating about this is that it didn't seem to matter whether Jesus saw the joy of those gathered at a wedding or the sorrow of those gathered at the funeral of a loved one. It didn't matter whether he saw his own mother or a prostitute. It didn't matter whether he saw a person of great wealth and power or a poor widow dropping her last coin in the box. It didn't really matter whether he saw his own disciples or his executioners. It didn't matter whether he saw a flower or a bird. Jesus saw God in all that he saw. And Jesus says to each of us "You have eyes to see but you do not see.[109]

But not only did Jesus see God in everything and everyone, Jesus' state of consciousness allowed him to see and know that he and God were completely united as one. He said, "The Father and I are one,"[110] and, "The one who has seen me has seen the Father."[111] Despite all appearance of separateness, and despite the fact that what he was claiming was judged by the Sadducees to be heretical, Jesus was unambiguous about the reality of his complete union with God.

Beyond this, Jesus' state of consciousness allowed him to recognize that in this regard, he was no different than any other person. Just listen to his words on this: "On that day you will know that I am in my Father, you are in me, and I am in you."[112] He saw all humans, not just those of his own religion (Judaism) as part of himself and ontologically "in God." This explains his radical inclusiveness as, for example, when he praised the faith of both the pagan Roman centurion and the pagan Canaanite woman as superior to those in his own faith tradition. Everything he encountered he saw through the eyes of his humanity and the state of consciousness that I am calling Kingdom consciousness. And what he longed for was that everyone would see and know the same truth by entering and living out of the same state of consciousness.

It was from this elevated platform of consciousness that Jesus answered the question of the Pharisees about the greatest commandment. Recall his words:

> Love the Lord your God with all your heart, with all your soul, and with all your mind. This is the greatest and most important command. The second is like it: Love your neighbour as yourself.[113]

The first of these two commandments seems understandable – even if the standard it sets is unimaginably high. The second, however, we usually misunderstand – reading it incorrectly as "Love your neighbour as you *love* yourself." But this is *not* what Jesus said. This commandment does not assume, as some suggest, self-love – then encouraging you to pass on this same sort of love to others. What Jesus actually asks is that we love others *as* ourselves.

In doing this, Jesus invites us to recognize our deep interconnectedness. We are all one in Christ. He is the vine and we are the branches.[114] Separateness is an illusion. Difference and uniqueness are real. But equally real is the fact that we are all integrally part of the whole that is Christ. We are all parts of one body – the body of Christ.[115]

The Kingdom of Heaven, in Cynthia Bourgeault's words, is *not* "a place you *go to*, but a place you *come from*. It is a whole new way of looking at the world, a transformed awareness that literally turns this world into a different place."[116] The Kingdom of heaven is the mind and consciousness of Christ – something that starts within but then leads to the transformation of the world as all things are made new in Christ.

The Mind of Christ

The second crucially important New Testament metaphor for transformation is making the mind of Christ our own. This brings us right to the heart of wisdom acquisition.

Paradoxically, the mind of Christ is something we already possess,[117] but must learn to access.[118] This means that our truest and deepest mind is, in reality, the mind of Christ. Wisdom comes when we learn to access this mind.

Some Christians understand making the mind of Christ their own in terms of adopting certain beliefs. Generally these will be whatever beliefs are counted most important in their church culture. But adopting a new mind has less to do with *what* we believe than with *how* we believe. Adopting a new mind involves a change of consciousness.

This invitation to a transformation of consciousness is a theme that we encounter throughout the New Testament. It is, however, quite understandable if you missed it. The reason it is so easily missed is that the Greek word involved – *metanoia* – is seriously mistranslated in most English Bibles. Literally meaning "beyond the mind," most Bibles follow the unfortunate mis-translation of St. Jerome's Latin Bible (the Vulgate) by rendering *metanoia* as "repent."[119] Think, for example, of the familiar words of Jesus immediately after his temptation in the wilderness: "Repent, for the kingdom of Heaven is close at hand."[120] Jesus was not urging repentance as an act of moral reform, or looking back in sorrow or contrition. He was urging us to receive a new, higher mind – not merely a superficial change *of* mind but the much more radical re-orientation of our total self that is arises from a transmutation of consciousness.[121]

[margin: ? so weak]

This becomes clear when we look at the two root words that form *metanoia: meta,* meaning "higher" and *noia* (from *noos*), meaning "mind." What Jesus was proclaiming was that if we wish to enter the kingdom of Heaven we need a higher mind, the higher level of consciousness that comes through awakening and transformation.

[margin: way too Greek totally misses context w/ John the Baptist]

If we are to know the Kingdom of Heaven as an inner reality we need nothing less than a transformed consciousness. This is what it takes to see through the heart and mind of Christ.

If Jesus were speaking to us in English today, I think he'd say something like the following:

> Wake up! Can't you see the Kingdom of Heaven that is springing into life all around you! If you can't, you need the updated mental operating system that is the very mind of God. This is what it means to enter the Kingdom of Heaven and to see and know through the mind of Christ. This is what it takes to see what God is doing to make all things new. And this is what it takes to

[margin: Now – he's been reading Richard Rohr (?) and who knows what]

participate in God's cosmic transformational plan. But it all starts with the transformation of your consciousness.

Acquiring the mind of Christ allows us to fully participate in the kingdom of God as a here-and-now reality, not just a hope for the future. This is not simply for Christians. We have no monopoly on the kingdom of God or the mind of Christ. Almost unbelievable, it is God's plan for all people and everything – a plan to make all things new and whole in Christ.

Transformation is the crucial word in describing this grand cosmic plan. It is the key to both accessing the mind of Christ and the wisdom that issues from it.

Learning to make the mind of Christ our own is the ultimate source of the wisdom we so desperately need to deal with the world's most pressing geo-political challenges. Seeing the world through the eyes of Christ is what we need if we are to truly learn to love our neighbor as our self. It is, therefore, what we desperately need in interpersonal and international relations. Seeing ourselves and our lives through the eyes of Christ is what we need to guide us. Nothing could be more important for not only our future but also for the future of the world.

Making Theology Practical

Neither beliefs nor understanding are enough for us to acquire the mind of Christ or fully inhabit the Kingdom of Heaven. It is, as I have said, the fruit of awakening and transformation.

In the next chapter we will talk about our part in that transformational process – what we can do to increase the chances of being awake when the light that illumines our hearts goes on. But to prepare us for that, let's take a moment to look at several practical implications of the theology we have been discussing in this chapter.

First, note that acquiring the mind of Christ is an internal process that subsequently changes how we act and live. But it starts with an inner awakening that, with grace and our consent, can become the series of a whole series of awakenings that eventually pull us past the tipping point and over the cliff of transformation.

> You can't cross a chasm by small steps. You have to let go and jump.

We cannot simply grow our way into living the wisdom of the mind of Christ by trying to think or act like Jesus. Although there is great value in the historic Christian practice of the imitation of Christ, accessing and living the wisdom of the mind of Christ requires a quantum shift in the core of our being. This doesn't come in some sort of trickle-down process as a result of changing our beliefs or behaviors. That puts the cart ahead of the horse.

But it is also important to recognize the non-linear nature of the process of acquiring the mind and consciousness of Christ. In fact, unlike growth, it isn't usually even gradual. The wisdom walk is not like ascending a mountain where slowly but surely, moment by moment, we see a larger vista. Wisdom acquisition is more like crossing a chasm than climbing a mountain. You can't cross a chasm by small steps. Instead you have to let go and jump. The letting go and jumping are essential components of the transformational journey and are, therefore, essential parts of wisdom acquisition.

Walking that path of wisdom acquisition is walking the path that Jesus walked. It is a path of life, death and resurrection – living with consent to the death of our small, egoic self and coming to newness of life in the truth of our self-in-Christ. This is how we not only access the mind of Christ but also allow it to flow through us.

This is not a path we can walk alone. Learning and living wisdom requires the support of others. We all need others for encouragement, modeling, and practical help in not allowing our awakened heart to go back to sleep. We also need the help of others in maintaining alignment with the creative Spirit of Wisdom who inhabits all of creation and who is our truest and deepest self.

However, we need more than a spiritual friend or companion. We need to be part of one or more communities that support transformation and that are themselves open to transformation. Such communities embrace change and have learned to continuously evolve. They encourage seeking rather than self-contented finding. And, most importantly, they offer limitless support without even a hint of constraint.[122]

Sadly, of course, this does not describe most churches, which, in the words of Richard Rohr, are more tribal than transformational. But churches are not the only forms of community that can support transformation and you need not limit yourself to one community.

For several decades my primary spiritual community has been widely dispersed. Mostly made up of people who have been part of retreats my wife and I have led around the world, it is now enlarged to include program participants in *Cascadia Living Wisdom School* where our engagement is through ongoing online interaction and videoconferences. You might wonder if this is really worthy of being called community. All I can say is that it is as real as any spiritual community I have ever experienced. And it meets all the criteria I have identified for supporting awakening and transformation.

Spiritual communities can take many forms. Churches are certainly one of these forms but if your church fails to meet the standards of support I have suggested, keep open to the other ways in which community can be created and experienced.

The transformational journey is costly and demanding. This is why we need to be held by others with boundless support that lacks any hint of constraint. We need this holding before, during and after the transitions that come as part of the journey because we need these people to help us acknowledge and grieve the losses and celebrate the new gifts and blessings. We need to journey with them as together we unfold and find our home in Christ and in the wisdom that flows from making Christ's mind and heart our own.

No one should embark on this journey without seriously counting the costs of walking this path. This is why Jesus placed so much emphasis on the cost of following him. But, of the many people who I have been privileged to accompany on this journey I know of no one who regrets having made it!

Pausing

to Ponder

---

1. *How would things change for you if living within the Kingdom of Heaven begins as a state of consciousness?*

2. *Return to Page 121 and reread the quote from James Finley where he describes what Jesus saw in everything and everyone he encountered. What would change in you if this were what you saw? Notice what stirs in your heart as you reflect on the fact that this same seeing and knowing is available for you.*

3. *What most struck you in the closing section of this chapter where I discussed some of the practical matters involved in walking the transformation path of wisdom acquisition? What do you most fear? What draws you forward with the most hope?*

Additional Reading and Things to Ponder

Edward J. Anton, *Repentance: A Cosmic Shift of Mind and Heart* (Waltham, MA: Discipleship Publications International, 2005). While this short book is now out of print it can still be found for sale, even sometimes as a free, downloadable PDF. As the sub-title indicates, it focuses on the quantum shift in mind and heart involved in *metanoia* when it is understood as taking on the mind of Christ.

17   Transformation: The Journey

It is easy to both glamorize and trivialize transformation. People speak of a walk in the forest, a good massage, or looking at a starry sky as transformational. But notice how seldom they describe pain, suffering or loss in the same terms. However, when an external experience forms part of what we later might fairly describe as a transformation it is much more likely that the experience was something that would never be chosen by anyone in his or her right mind.

Transformation is an inner process, nor merely an inevitable response to an outer experience. It's an inner journey on which the person that begins the journey is not the same as the person who ends it.

Like any journey, transformation happens over an extended period of time. It is not an afternoon walk. Nor is like being zapped. It always involves a process – or from the perspective of the person in the midst of that process, it always involves a journey. It is a journey that is almost always involves suffering, loss, inner turmoil, disorientation, collapse and surrender.

Transformation may or may not have any apparent external triggering experience. Paul's conversion experience on the road to Damascus may have seemed to have occurred in a single blinding flash but the soil must always be prepared and the inner response to awakening offered with consent, not simply resignation.[123]

While the journey requires a lot of us, transformation is not a transactional process. We do not access wisdom as part of a cosmic deal we make with God in which wisdom comes as the pay-off for something we offer in exchange. But, we do have a crucial role to play in opening ourselves to the grace of transformation.

Our Part in the Process

We have already talked about of faith as an important feature of our part in the process. The good news about this is that while faith is something we need to exercise we are not required to create it. Like all good things, faith comes to us as a gift from God. But like all good gifts, faith is to be used, not stored. We

> Faith is to be used, not stored.

cultivate our faith by exercising it. And we exercise our faith in God by trusting God enough to remain open to whatever comes to us as part of the journey.

Awakenings are always accompanied by at least a brief opening in our inner self. This is the crack that allows us to receive the light that shines into the darkness of our slumbering non-wakefulness.

It begins with a moment of illumination that we notice in either our head or our heart. It might be exposure to a broader theological framework that suddenly opens the windows of our minds and fills us with light and expansiveness. Or it could start with a momentary but profound sense of awe in response to a fleeting glimpse of the interconnectedness of everything. But if it is an authentic awakening it will never be contained within either our head or heart. It is starts as mental illumination we must allow it to lead to a subsequent opening in our hearts. And if it starts as a heart illumination we must nurture its translation into an opening in our heads. We don't have to create those subsequent openings. All we need to do is respond to the awakening with hospitality and faith, watching as it then begins to cascade throughout our being.

Receiving gifts of at least momentary openness with hospitality is the way we offer our consent to further awakening and illumination. We do this by resisting the urge to understand what is happening to us while still remaining open to the illumination. Our hearts tell us that what is happening within us is precious and trustworthy. They tell us that God is in it. And we exercise our faith in God by remaining open to that which we do not understand but to which we offer our consent.

Pondering what is happening within us is not the same as trying to figure it out. Mental pondering invites heart pondering, just as heart pondering invites head pondering. Either one will increase openness, and both together create even more inner spaciousness.

Every awakening also contains a hidden invitation and responding to these invitations with consent prepares us for deeper awakening and eventual transformation. For example, the invitation may be as simple as a new level of desire to be more trusting, more loving, less controlled or less attached to one's beliefs or to the illusory certainty that they offer. Responding with consent to this means doing something. This might start as a very small inner action but it then needs to be translated into outer behavior.

Awakenings are not simply an insight, even a brilliant one. Nor are they ever simply an inner experience, even a profound one. Awakenings are bursts of awareness that come with disruptive energy. This is the energy that we mobilize when we respond to the invitation they carry. But even when we do, the energy is disruptive. Holding the tension of that disruption is one of the ways in which we exercise our faith.

Anything that exercises our faith and supports our openness and surrender is a spiritual exercise that will strengthen our faith. The Christian spiritual practices that have the most transformational potential are those with a contemplative dimension. This is because they are the ones that are grounded in stillness before self and God and that teach us the possibilities of wordless and thoughtless presence. It is in this practice of presence that we best learn openness and are given opportunities to practice surrender.

> Contemplation is apprehension that is uncluttered by thought.

Contemplation is not thinking about things. Contemplation is apprehension that is uncluttered by thought – particularly preconception and analysis. At its core it is the practice of openness to the flow of the present moment. This openness is essential for transformation as it allows us to step back from the ordinary background noise of consciousness. It allows us to notice our pre-occupations and identifications and then gently release them and whatever else is in our awareness. The goal is not to eliminate anything but to release everything. This is the essence of the radical practice of contemplation.

Surrender lies right at the core of our part of the transformational process. The journey follows a path of descent that ultimately leads to death – the death of our small ego-self. Resurrection is only possible after death and it is only on the other side of the total collapse of our ego-self that we discover our true larger self-in-Christ.

Margaret Silf paints a wonderful word picture of the way in which deconstruction is followed by reconstruction and transcendence:

> "I see myself standing on the banks of a fast-flowing river. I know I must cross, but there is no bridge. Then a figure, a Christ-figure, comes to me carrying a large boulder, and places it in front of me, in the river, inviting me to take a step out onto it. Every day he brings another boulder, another stepping stone. Every day I move farther into the waters, balancing precariously on my fragile faith. One day he is late. I turn around, mid-river, and only then do I see where the boulders are coming from. He is systematically deconstructing my cozy little cottage on the shore, in order to turn it into stepping stones for my onward journey. He is using my past to create my future. He is asking me to reach out with both hands – one to let go of all I thought I couldn't live without, and one to reach toward everything I thought I could never attain."[124]

Transformation demands a deconstruction of our past so everything can be included and is put together in a new way. Ultimately, we do not need to leave any part of our self behind as all things become new. And paradoxically, just as Jesus said, this only happens when we let go of the self we presently are – even to the point of being willing to lose that self. Only then can we discover and become the true and full self that we are in Christ.

Markers on the Journey

The transformational journey is an ongoing journey of awakenings and new, ever-deepening levels of deconstruction and reconstruction. But it isn't endless. It does have a destination and we can identify markers on the journey.

We know we are on the right path when we begin to see God everywhere – in others, in the world, in ourselves, and in life. The medieval nun, Mechtild of Magdeburg (c. 1212—c. 1282) described this in these words: "The day of my spiritual awakening was the day I saw and I saw all things in God and God in all things."[125]

Meister Eckhart suggests that this awareness of the larger realities in which we are held is the core of spiritual transformation. He described it as the advent of Christ-awareness or, the birth of God in the soul. It involves the dawning awareness that while our own being has a center outside of itself in God, God's being also has a corresponding center in us. It is the birth of new knowing that is grounded in new seeing – what we might call mystical vision and knowing. Nothing is a clearer sign of the expansion of consciousness that is part of transformation.

Accompanying this transformation of consciousness is an expansion and transformation of identity. We usually first experience this as a softening of boundaries between self and non-self. Others lose their otherness as

we see them and us as deeply connected in Christ. Once we begin to
see this we recognize the mystical truth that although I am not you, I
am not fundamentally other than you and, although you are not me,
you are not fundamentally other than me. From this larger perspective
of seeing through the eyes of Christ we recognize differences but not
separateness. We recognize, not just believe, that in Christ there is
neither Jew nor Greek, male nor female for we are all one.[126]

Recognizing God's home in us and ours in God opens us to recognizing
God not just in the world in some static sense but in the very flow of
life, moment by moment. This then allows us to pass on the flow of love
to others, not simply hoard it.

> The purpose of transformation is transpersonal, not merely personal.

As we begin to experience the
freedom of being part of this
cosmic flow we will also begin to
experience lessening attachment
to opinions, experiences,
certainty, reputation, and
everything else we had been
clutching close to our chest.
We will also begin to notice that
we are less willful and more willing – more characterized by consent
than opposition or striving to make something happen. Another way of
saying this is that we begin to experience ourselves as increasingly free
of attachments and reactivity and free, therefore, for true engagement
and non-reactive response to people and issues.

And with freedom and increased love comes increased humility. Previous
certainties drop away with other forms of brittleness and rigidity. In

their place come an acceptance of truth wherever it is found and an increased capacity to hold the tensions of reality.

The journey of transformation is a journey into God. The whole point of this journey is a return to our true home so that we can fully participate in God's cosmic agenda of making all things new and whole in Christ. The purpose of transformation is transpersonal, not merely personal. Seeing our place in the larger whole allows us to move out into the world as a better conduit of love. This, not perfection or fulfillment, is the point of transformation.

Speaking Personally

I know these things are possible. I have seen enough evidence of transformation in others and experienced enough of it myself to have no hesitation or reservation in making that claim.

I do, however, hesitate to speak of my own experience, as I don't want to suggest that I have arrived or that this process is anywhere near complete in me. But because I am deeply aware of the fact that transformation is not an accomplishment but a gift, in the spirit of transparency I am prepared to share something of my own awakenings and the transformational component of my own journey. I do this to illustrate some of the process that I have described here and in earlier chapters.

Like most people, I have slept through vastly more potential awakenings than those I have responded to with consent. But I have also had a number of moments of significant awakening. And I have experienced disorientation and terror associated with them – particularly when they began to cascade before I was ready to let go and float in the Dark River of Love that swept me away from my safe controlled life.

My first major awakening was at age 35. To all external appearances my life was going well – both personally and professionally. But internally, I realized I was facing a spiritual and existential crisis. I felt forced to acknowledge that I was profoundly tired of being a Christian – or at least, of being the kind of Christian I was. I was bored with a life of faith that involved little more than belief and belonging. It wasn't that I doubted the content of my faith but I was tired of convictions and certainty. I felt a profound longing to know God, not simply know *about* God – and to know myself, others and everything in the depths of my being not merely within the shallowness of my mind. And I knew that if I did not respond to this longing for something more I would suffer profound soul damage. I had no idea where hospitality to the longings and dissatisfactions would lead me, but I chose to take the leap and see.

Over the next several years, this led me to a number of incredible gifts and other significant awakenings. Ecumenical explorations within the Eastern Orthodox tradition led me to the Jesus Prayer and the Prayer of Quiet – these Hesychastic practices leading me to a place of deep engagement with both my body and my unconscious mind in prayer. Together, these became extremely potent fuel for deeper personal integration.

I was also blessed to be able to work closely with Fr. Basil Pennington during these years. He introduced me to Centering Prayer and to a large number of Catholic mystics.

During this period my wife – Juliet Benner - also played an extremely important role in helping me remain open and responsive to the leading of the Spirit. Trained as an Ignatian Spiritual director and possessing a deep and rich understanding of the wisdom of Ignatian spirituality, Juliet led me through the year-long version of the Ignatian Spiritual Exercises, something that served as a particularly powerful context for further awakenings.

My next major awakening began about a decade after this and continued for several decades after it. Work with Taoism, Buddhism and Islam formed the context of the next set of transformational tipping points. However, describing this as work obscures the fact that friendships were central to this engagement. They also ensured that this was not just a mental exercise but one that engaged the totality of my being.

There is no question that this interfaith exposure profoundly deepened my roots and grounding in Christianity. As strange as it may sound, it was in this context that I truly began to know the reality of Christ in me and me in Christ. Building on the mystical knowing that had begun in my work with the Christian mystics, the experience of praying with those of other faiths had an incredibly powerful impact on me. It remains today singularly precious.

But the changes in my inner world during this period became the cause of enormous pain and disruption as it led to fierce attack from the most conservative elements of my readers, friends, and acquaintances. While I had by this point stopped direct involvement with evangelical institutions I had left on good terms and happily considered evangelicals my brothers and sisters in Christ. The attacks I was soon to experience made very clear that those feelings were far from universally shared by those within the tradition I had left.

The trigger for the attacks apparently was my openness to other religions, and the audacity I had evidently shown in daring to speak of the ways in which my faith had been deepened and enriched through engagement with them. Suddenly I was attacked by a number of people who felt that not only did they have to publically identify me as a heretic but also to do everything they could to silence me.

The depth of their hatred was astounding until I realized how deeply threatened they were by the broader vistas and freedom my words and life reflected. But it was still horrendous to experience. Although I had more previous experience with deep personal wounding through betrayals than I would ever wish on anyone I had never encountered such devastating levels of venomous rage. Thankfully, however, my sense of being Christian and my commitment to following Christ was deeper than ever before. I took comfort in the realization that this was part of what it means to share the sufferings of Christ.

Thankfully, this was not the last chapter. Removing myself even further from communities of exclusion and judgment and finding my spiritual home in more supportive places I was able to continue my journey and experience further awakenings and transformational shifts in consciousness and identity. I will mention only one – an early moment in what has been a series of powerful moments of mystical knowing.

It happened during a foggy, early morning walk by the ocean on Vancouver Island in British Columbia, Canada. Here is the poem that poured out of me when I returned home several hours later:

It Happened Again

It happened again,
This morning, as I walked the sea wall,
Smelling the salt in the mist as it rolled across the Strait
From the deeper waters off the other shore.

My heart was filled with gratitude
And joy.
But that was not what happened.

Suddenly I felt overwhelming waves of Love.

For a moment I knew with startling certainty
That God was present,
That I was in God, and that God was in me.

I knew that we were not alone, not orphans.

I knew
That Love was in the world, at work,
Making all things new.

And then as suddenly, ordinary knowing returned.
But I remember.
That is enough.

This was not the first time I had a moment of mystical knowing. Nor was it the last. But, while equally fleeting, this moment immediately became a knowing that remains with me today as powerfully as it did in that instant on the breakwater, in the fog, at dawn many years ago. I am more certain of what I came to know in that moment than I am of anything else I might claim to know by any other means.

> Moments of mystical knowing are not as important as remembering and trusting what they reveal.

I am far from continuously in the state of altered consciousness that momentarily I was blessed to experience that morning, but the knowing that it offered has become a stable part of my background awareness.

Ordinary knowing is still occasionally interrupted by moments of mystical knowing. But, those moments of mystical knowing are not as important to me as remembering and trusting what they reveal.

I am far from finished this transformational journey. But I have tasted enough to know that our sense of being a separate self is an illusion. I know that we are all part of a larger, interconnected whole that I name as Christ. This knowing of the interconnectedness of everything in existence is the foundation of any wisdom I have managed to access. I know there is much more yet to access and thankful that my journey is not yet over.

Pausing

to Ponder

1. *Think of any awakenings you have experienced and consider what your part was in the process. What part did faith play in the process?*

2. *What helps you be more open in your head and heart? What role do contemplative spiritual practices play in supporting this openness?*

3. *What helps you cultivate a life of surrender? What have you known to this point in your journey of the collapse of your small ego-self and what role, if any, did consent play in that process?*

4. *In this chapter I described the deconstruction and disorientation that forms part of awakenings and transformation. What part did these things play in the major hinges of your journey?*

5. *What, if any, moments of mystical knowing have you experienced? What role did they play in your awakening and transformation? How do you respond to the priority I suggested on the mystical*

knowing over the actual experience? What do you know based on subjective experience that would be hard to defend rationally?

Additional Readings and Things to Ponder

Phileena Heuertz, *Pilgrimage of a Soul: Contemplative Spirituality for the Active Life, Revised Edition* (Downers Grove, IL: InterVarsity Press, 2017). This deeply personal account of a pilgrimage to the tomb of St. James in Spain becomes for the author a framework for discussing the pilgrimage of the soul on the journey of awakening and transformation. Read with head and heart it is deeply instructive and powerfully helpful.

Part Three   Living Wisdom

In Part Three we explore what it means to live with wisdom. How might seeing through the eyes of the mind and heart of Christ change our way of being in the world? What would be different if we truly knew our deep connectedness to all of humanity, to the earth and to the universe? These are the sorts of questions we will address as we reflect on how wisdom translates into behavior, then into habits, and finally into a stable lifestyle.

"The wisdom that comes from heaven is first of all pure; then peace-loving, considerate, submissive, full of mercy and good fruit, impartial and sincere."
James 3:17

18   From Theory to Practice

Wisdom is not a faucet to be turned on only when facing important decisions. It is far too precious to be relegated to such a small segment of your life.

Wisdom is meant to flow into the totality of your existence – and then out through you, into the world. If it doesn't flow like this, it is nothing more than knowledge. All authentic wisdom is, therefore, living wisdom. If it isn't being lived it isn't wisdom.

This does not mean that a person with wisdom is always wise. As we saw earlier, wise people still often do incredibly stupid things. But a person who has begun to rely on the inner compass and compassion that come from having acquired the consciousness and heart of Christ is a person who will be living in ways that increasingly reflect wisdom.

Translating Knowing into Living

New ways of seeing and knowing do not automatically flow into new ways of behaving and being.

I think, for example, of people who were born blind but healed of their blindness as adults. Describing the enormity of the challenge such people face when compared to those of us who were born sighted, neurologist, Oliver Sachs notes that whereas an infant merely learns to see and then naturally adjusts everything else to this information, a newly sighted adult has to undergo radical reorganization of information processing and responding that flies in the face of a lifetime of experience.[127] Often they feel overwhelmed, and resentful of the disruption to their life that the healing brings. Their new "gift" of sight does not in any way automatically translate into welcome or useful vision.

I also think of astronauts who return to earth deeply impacted by the experience of viewing earth from space. Frequently they speak of returning with a feeling of awe for the planet, a profound understanding of the interconnection of all life, and a renewed sense of responsibility for taking care of earth.[128]

Col. Chris Hadfield, a Canadian astronaut who served as commander of the International Space Station and completed three space missions, spoke of this in a conversation with one of our *Cascadia Living Wisdom School* program participants. He described looking at earth from space as an overwhelming experience of "galactic light entering planetary eyes." Earth gazing, he said, was far from a contemplative experience. It involved "an ecstatic build-up of energy that felt like it was bursting forward into being." Something new was emerging. He knew he had to live in ways that honoured what was being born in him.[129]

I have often seen the same thing in people responding to spiritual awakenings – a sense of having just turned a major corner in the journey of life but being profoundly unaware of how to respond to what has been received and is now seen and known. Disorientation and hesitation is quite common, as is a sense of needing help from others in making sense of the experience.

Perhaps this was why immediately following his encounter with Christ on the road to Damascus, the Apostle Paul spent several days in disorienting blindness before Ananias laid his hands on him and restored his sight. However, after recovering his sight and being baptized he then spent even more time with the disciples before being ready to walk the path that was suggested by his new sight and new knowing.[130] This illustrates the crucial role of community in learning how to respond to the new seeing and understanding that emerges from acquiring the consciousness of Christ. It takes others who understand your experience to help you learn how to walk in the light of what you see.

> If you are attentive, your heart will guide your response to an awakening.

But taking those first steps is crucial, even if they are only baby steps. Just as faith becomes real when it begins to translate into action so too wisdom becomes real when it begins to express itself in behavior.

As I have said before, the seeds of those first steps lie in the awakening itself. If you are attentive to it, your heart will guide your response. It may be an invitation to let love flow more freely and fully through you, or possibly to take more concrete steps in reaching out to the marginalized and disenfranchised in the world. Or you may feel called to get more involved politically as a way to leverage larger systemic changes. Or, perhaps you will feel impelled to get involved with local groups working on important global issues.

For many the call is for more active care of the earth. This could start with stopping all unavoidable use of plastics in packaging. Or it might begin with a desire to live with a smaller carbon footprint or reduced levels of consumption. Or, it could start with more responsible use of energy.

But don't read this list as prescriptive. There is no one right place to start, no single way in which wisdom should manifest itself. Just start doing something in response to what you have seen and now know. And allow the Spirit of Wisdom to guide you once you have started moving.

Numinous Encounters

Often people get drawn into making grand plans about how they want to live the rest of their life after an awakening. They know that something important has happened in their depths but fall into the trap of trying to control, understand and manage it. But these egoic ways of responding simply sabotage the potential of the sacred new life that is beginning to gestate within their depths.

Every awakening is a numinous encounter – a brush with the divine. Moses shows us an alternative to engaging these encounters strategically.

While tending sheep in the wilderness Moses suddenly saw a burning bush that, inexplicably, was not being consumed. Eager to understand this strange thing he began to approach the fire, full of curiosity. Immediately, God called out to him from the bush and warned him to come no closer but take off his shoes because he was on holy ground. Moses did as God asked, and in so doing he moved beyond curiosity to reverence and became able to recognize and respond to the divine presence that was the at the heart of his awakening.[131]

Recognizing that every awakening is a numinous encounter helps us in the same way as it helped Moses. We too need to avoid the default, take-charge responses that quickly desacralize these moments. We too need to learn to stand in awe, to listen and watch as the presence of the Spirit reveals itself and then reveals our most appropriate personal response.

> Awe leads to action when we notice the Divine Presence in an awakening.

Responding to an awakening by turning it into a project serves the ego well but will always trouble the heart. Something in our depths knows better than to follow the siren call to manage these experiences that are beyond comprehension.

Wisdom is accessed by following the heart. Deeply oriented toward the sacred, awe is its first line of response to numinous encounters. Once awe begins to resonate within our heart it will lead us to the most appropriate action.

Habits of the Heart

Responses to awakenings that are shaped by the heart have a very different character than those shaped by the mind or will. They are less forceful, but certainly not less powerful. They are also less rigid and they call less attention to themselves. Rather than being pushed by compulsion or conviction they flow out of our depths as an expression of our values.

It is hard to talk about wisdom without talking about values. This is why wisdom must be desired, not merely sought as a curiosity. Wisdom shapes values which, in turn, become habits – habits that Alexis de Tocqueville called habits of the heart.[132]

Habits of the heart provide inner scaffolding for behaviors to coalesce around and then begin to guide life. Isolated wisdom practices – things such as, for example, living with less so that others may simply live or caring for the environment – can become organizing principles of being that both shape and express character. Much more than simply serving as guides to living they become the framework for ways of being. Habits of the heart make and express who we are – as persons, communities, even as nations. [133]

But remember, habits are not where we start in living wisdom. We start with the baby steps of responding to the invitations that come to us as part of our awakening. We start with the nudges in our hearts that we will notice if we are attentive to what is happening within our depths, not simply in our minds or in the world.

Habits build around patterns in these responses that develop over time. So, be prepared to give your living wisdom time to develop. Don't allow it to become a project. Just listen to your heart and respond with consent.

In the next three chapters we will examine some of the major ingredients that tend to form part of living wisdom. However, please do not misunderstand them as a list of recommendations to build a wisdom lifestyle. Instead, take them as examples of common ways of responding to seeing through the eyes of Christ, remembering that your incarnation of Living Wisdom should be as unique as you are as a person. It will be unusual, however, if it doesn't include a response to the issues to which we now turn.

Pausing

to Ponder

1. *Notice again the invitations to live in new ways that were part of any recent awakenings or illuminations you have your received. How have you responded to these invitations?*

2. *For you, what has kept new ways of seeing and knowing from flowing into new ways of behaving and being?*

3. *What do you know of the difference between doing things with an attachment to outcome versus the freedom of doing things from a place of non-attachment? What invitations to live with more of that freedom do you experience in reflecting on this difference?*

. What are your defining habits of the heart – things that express your deepest values and shape your way of being in the world? If you find it hard to identify these for yourself, talk with someone who knows you well about this question and get their help in knowing yourself in these terms.

Additional Readings and Things to Ponder

For more on the astronauts' life-changing experience of seeing Earth from space, watch the short film documentary film, The Overview Effect: https://vimeo.com/55073825

If you wish to follow this further, you might enjoy a short article discussing the same phenomenon: *National Geographic Magazine*, "They Saw Earth From Space: Here's How it Changed Them," March 28, 2018, https://www.nationalgeographic.com/magazine/2018/03/astronauts-space-earth-perspective/

19   Stewardship of the Earth . . . and Beyond

Seeing through the eyes of an awakened heart and transformed consciousness always produces changes in how we perceive ourselves in relation to everything else – other people, God, the earth, even the cosmos. These changes often start with a changed sense of our relationship to the earth and that will be our focus in this chapter.

From Mother Earth to the Environment

For all but the last few centuries, humans have lived with a deep sense of connection to nature. We knew that we were part of the earth, not simply creatures inhabiting it. We knew that the earth was alive and formed the vital ground of our existence. And we knew it was sacred.

Anthropologists tell us that the sacredness of nature forms the backdrop of the mythologies of all cultures of the world. [134] The gods and goddess that populate these myths had their origins in nature. They were ways of acknowledging that we existed within a fragile web of life and that we faced forces that were beyond our control. Recognizing earth as our sacred mother, our ancestors acknowledged both the power of nature and also our dependence on it.

> We have become beings who live on earth but are not part of it.

This all began to change profoundly with the rise of scientific rationalism in the eighteenth century. Suddenly, our subjective but intimate knowing *of* the world was replaced by an objective knowing *about* it. But this involved assuming the position of outside observers. We lost our intimate encounter with the earth and we became beings who lived *on* the earth but who were not *of* it.

Ripping ourselves out of the living fabric of the web of life, we imagined ourselves as if we were looking at the world from a distance. But, in the words of Bruce Sanguin, "This dualism has enabled us to imagine that the earth belongs to us, when the bio-spiritual truth is that in every way conceivable, we belong to the earth."[135] And tragically, once we began to think that the earth belonged to us as something separate from us, it became possible to exploit and plunder it. It is much harder (although not, of course, impossible) to exploit and plunder family than those to whom you experience no attachment.

Suddenly all we were left with was an environment to be managed and a planet to be largely ignored. Christians were reminded of our responsibility to be good stewards of creation. But, looked at more carefully, perhaps it's time to acknowledge that stewardship – at least as we have understood and, at the best, practiced it – has been more part of the problem than the solution.

> The story of cosmology is the story of the world's mystics.

Between Stories

Thomas Berry tells us that humans are presently living between two great stories of life – the story of religion and the story of science.[136] Both religious and scientific fundamentalists have approached these stories in a reductionist way that is burdened with prejudices and misunderstandings. Consequently, they see only contradictions and tensions.

However, those who have listened to these stories with an open heart and mind have recognized the profound way in which they complement each other. In fact, the emerging consensus of those who follow the story of science, particularly recent developments in physics and cosmology, is that science now offers a profound confirmation of the deep story of religion.

Judy Cannato writes:

> During the last several decades, a new story has indeed emerged, a new cosmology that brings matters of science and matters of faith into a space where they no longer need collide, but can complement each other and render a fuller picture of what is true. Ironically, in modern times it is science that has told us the story of how all life is connected in a fundamental way—a story that the world's mystics have been telling for centuries.[137]

Christians have also very much been caught in this same gap between stories, but they have faced a second complication. They have been caught between the two creation stories that are told in Genesis[138] –

generally unaware of the important difference between them and failing to see their quite different implications for our relationship to the earth.

The second creation story is the more familiar one and the one that has behind the Christian notion of ecological stewardship. In it, humans are given dominion over the animals and responsibility for subduing nature. Just as colonialism was, at the time, understood as a story of benevolence, so too we have viewed this dominion and stewardship story in the same positive way. We have been told that our job is to be a good landlord. But the point is that when we are landlords who are removed from the land we become distant landlords. Rather than being part of nature we stand over it. As the story of colonialism makes clear, management that might be intentionally benevolent always runs the risk of exploitation when it is offered at a distance.

In the first creation story the role of humans is to tend the garden of nature. Bruce Sanguin describes what this involves. "The act of tending a garden, as any gardener knows, involves loving attention. Frequent strolls through the garden are mandatory, just to check in with what's happening. What's coming up? Which plants are crowding out the others . . . A relationship is established in which the garden silently communicates its needs and desires, to those with ears to hear."

Good gardeners are intimately involved with plants and soil as they tend the garden. If they are wise, they don't force their plan on the creative process. They facilitate the unfolding rather than attempt to engineer it. No matter how hard you try or how badly you want to make it happen you just can't grow orchids outdoors in Canada or maple trees in the deserts of Saudi Arabia.

Tending rather than willful managing is the wisdom way of nature. And it's the wisdom way of humans who want to align with the Spirit of God as it animates, renews and draws everything in creation toward its fullness in Christ.

Beyond Anthropocentrism

Both the earth and humans will only survive if humans stop exploiting and learn to identify and intimately commune with the natural world.

> Replacing exploitation with communion.

Communing is part of tending. It is possible to manage something from a distance without communion but it is impossible to tend the well-being of anything or anyone without it.

Communing involves coming alongside. It demands respect. And it requires abandoning the arrogance of our self-centeredness. In relation to the world, it involves what Thomas Berry calls a movement from anthropocentrism to ecocentrism.[139]

Quite simply, the world does not revolve around us. We need to once again take our rightful place within nature and then cooperate with God's agenda of making everything in existence whole. This is the blueprint behind the dynamic unfolding of the universe.

Ecocentrism involves more than changed behavior. It involves a profound shift in our identity and consciousness that comes from reconnecting our apparently separate selves with nature and discovering a previously unimaginable kinship with all of life. It involves a shift from the skin-encapsulated ego to a wider construct of identity that philosopher, Arne Naess has called the ecological self.[140]

Two things play an important role as first steps toward this movement from our skin-encapsulated ego to a larger ecological self – begining to join others in taking concrete actions to slow damage to earth and its inhabitants, and spending regular time in nature.

Concrete actions to slow the damage to the earth and its inhabitants is not just about changing the world but also ourselves. Don't wait until you feel you have somehow grown into a wholely new ecological self. That will not happen if you do not begin to take concrete steps to respond to the wisdom you already possess. Start anywhere – but start! Get involved with people who are moving in the same direction as you, both in your community and more globally. Read, get informed and inspired, and learn with others. But, most importantly, act on the basis of what you know. This will not only begin to slow damage to earth and its inhabitants but also to heal you. Gradually it allow you to access the wisdom that is both embedded in nature and is at the core of your deepest self.

Spending time in nature may sound trivial in relation to things like engaging with others to try and shift patterns of water usage, deforestation, fossil-fuel dependence, behavior that led to extinction of plant and animal species, use of plastics, depletion of the ozone layer of the atmosphere, or many other things. But, each complements the other. Of course, concrete actions are urgent and essential. But the beauty of taking such actions is that they lead not just to the healing of the planet but to the healing of our own souls. In the same way, spending time in nature with openess of heart and soul will reinforce our commitment to active engagement with the world and its most important problems.

The wisdom of nature can't be understood by our minds. We have to actually experience it if we are to allow it speak to us through our hearts and bodies.

Thomas Berry suggests we need to engage nature with our senses. We need to learn to be present to the wind and the stars, to see the moon and the mountains, to hear the forests and rivers. He goes on:

> We especially need to hear the creatures of Earth before it is too late, before their voices are stilled forever through extinction occurring at such a rapid rate. Once gone they will never be heard again. Extinction is forever. The divine experience they communicate will never again be available to humans. A dimension of the human soul will never be activated as it might have been. Nothing can replace what we are losing . . . We have lost sight of the fact that these myriad creatures are revelations of the divine and inspirations to our spiritual life.[141]

Christocentric, not Just Ecocentric

But perhaps you are wondering where God is in all this talk about Mother Earth and the movement from anthropocentrism to ecocentrism. Perhaps this is a good time to remind ourselves that all of creation, not just humans, is a divine manifestation.

Long before the birth of Jesus, the first incarnation happened approximately 14 billion years ago at a moment scientists call the Big Bang. Richard Rohr suggests we call this the First Manifestation because it was the point when God first materialized and revealed the God self."[142] As expressed in an ancient Islamic teaching, it is as if in the act of creation God says, "I was a hidden treasure and longed to be known and so I created the world."[143] Creation was an act of Divine self-expression, the pouring out of the God-self into the universe, the first infusing of spirit within matter.

> Creation was the translation of the score into the music.

In her wonderful book, *The Body of God,* Christian theologian Sallie McFague argues that earth herself is an embodiment of the divine. That is why earth is sacred. God's presence on earth is not limited to the moment and place of the birth of Jesus in Bethlehem two thousand years ago. God is present in all matter. God is incarnated in the world. As Sallie McFague puts it:

God is closer to us than we are to ourselves, for God is the breath or spirit that gives life to the billions of different bodies that make up God's body. But God is also the source, power, and goal of everything that is, for the creation depends utterly upon God.[144]

Cynthia Bourgeault suggests that this means that the universe is not simply an object created by God out of the effluence of love but is that love itself, made manifest. She goes on: "The created realm is not an artifact but an instrument through which the divine life becomes perceptible to itself. It's the way the score gets transformed into the music."[145]

Ecocentrism finds its fullest development in Christocentrism. Christ consciousness brings with it the orientation to earth as the body of God. It brings with it the consciousness that, in the words of Thomas Berry, the universe is composed of subjects to be communed with, not objects to be exploited.[146] It brings with it the awareness that I am a sibling to everything and everyone even as we are all together held in existence in Christ.

Once we truly begin to see the world through these eyes, hallowing of the earth in all its diversity of forms becomes a spiritual practice that bubbles up from a heart that is flooded with awe for the diversity of ways in which the presence of God permeates creation.

Wisdom gets practical once we see things as they really are. But, in the words of Bruce Sanguin, instead of hallowing earth, we hallow laissez-faire economics and sacrifice the planet on its altar. He goes on:

> Recognizing the planet as a manifestation of Spirit, and therefore also its sacred character, is the first step toward relinquishing whatever gets in the way of our hallowing. As part of this discipline, we will ask ourselves whether our lifestyles are aligned with this hallowing. Do we buy local produce, or do we eat vegetables trucking across the country, adding to the carbon levels of the atmosphere? Do the cars we drive honor the sacred nature of the planet? Do we invest in companies who try to reduce their ecological footprint? Do we use household products that are

toxic? Does our work, our vocation, contribute to the 'Great Work' of repairing the planet, or at least not impede her recovery?[147]

Once our identity begins to shift from being a steward of earth to being a manifestation of God who inhabits a planet that is itself a manifestation of its Source, things begin to change. We begin to experience the passion that we need to fuel and sustain us for the great work of repairing our planet. And once we begin to see ourselves very literally grounded in God in this way, we cannot help but see the whole of our life differently.

Pausing
to Ponder

1. How do you assess your relationship to the earth? How connected to it do you feel? What do you do to maintain that sense of connection?

2. How have you been making sense of the two great stories of science and religion?

3. Which of the two Biblical creation stories has most influenced how you relate to the world? What other differences or implications do you sense as you reflect on the difference between tending to the garden of earth versus exercising dominion over it and being a good steward of its resources?

4. *What sense does it make to you to speak of communing and identifying with nature? What emerges in your heart as you reflect on the notion of creation as the first incarnation and, therefore, a manifestation of God?*

5. *Take a moment and reflect on the quote from Bruce Sanguin about the implications of hallowing earth rather than lasses-faire economics:*

> "Recognizing the planet as a manifestation of Spirit, and therefore also its sacred character, is the first step toward relinquishing whatever gets in the way of our hallowing. As part of this discipline, we will ask ourselves whether our lifestyles are aligned with this hallowing. Do we buy local produce, or do we eat vegetables trucking across the country, adding to the carbon levels of the atmosphere? Do the cars we drive honor the sacred nature of the planet? Do we invest in companies who try to reduce their ecological footprint? Do we use household products that are toxic? Does our work, our vocation, contribute to the "Great Work" of repairing the planet, or at least not impede her recovery?"

How do you respond to the implications he identified? What others would you add to his list?

Additional Readings and Things to Ponder

For more on the theology of earth as a divine manifestation, read Sallie McFague, *The Body of God: An Ecological Theology*, (Fortress Press: 1993).

For more on the recent convergence of the stories of science and religion the work of evolutionary cosmologist, Brian Swimme, is singularly helpful. His books can be reviewed at https://www.amazon.com/Brian-Swimme/e/B001ITYQ1G while his award-winning video products are most easily be explored and accessed on the website of *The Center for the Story of the Universe* - http://storyoftheuniverse.org/

For an excellent discussion of the challenge of slowing and eventually reversing damage to the earth, I recommend Thomas Berry, *The Great Work: Our Way into the Future* (Three Rivers Press: 1999).

20   Money, Possessions and Attachments

Authentic living of wisdom can never be restricted to simply one domain of life. If it is real, wisdom will begin to spill out into all of life. This does not mean, however, that the flow of wisdom into all domains of our life will be easy. In this chapter we come to the place where we frequently offer the most resistance to wisdom – our money and possessions. The real issue, as we will see, is neither the money or the possessions but our attachments.

One of the first books I wrote on spirituality was also a book about wisdom.[148] However, the book contained not even a single reference to spirituality or wisdom. It was a book on the psychology of money and the publisher I wrote it for was a secular publisher of books on business and finance. That seemed to me to be a perfect platform for a book about the foolishness of our ways of relating to money and the possibilities of true financial freedom that are not dependent on how much we have but how we relate to what we have.

> Wisdom will always seem subversive to the systems that are dependent on foolishness.

The book did not get much attention because the publisher declared bankruptcy shortly after it was released. However, reader feedback and book reviews were generally positive. One reviewer, however, was quite ambivalent. After noting several things he appreciated he added a *caveat emptor* – buyer beware. He said the book was subversive because, by questioning the wisdom of consumerism and greed, it presented a serious challenge to capitalism and the entire modern way of life.

It seems he got my point. And his reaction is understandable. Wisdom will always seem subversive to the systems that are dependent on our foolishness!

Money is not the problem. Nor was it for Jesus. His warning was about the *love* of money, not money itself.[149] The issue is how we relate to our money – our attachment to it - and how we use it.

From a wisdom point of view, perhaps the central issue is how we deal with the commercial systems that are dependent on our remaining active consumers in order to fuel the economic engines of our societies.

I am keenly aware that some people will bristle on reading this. They might feel that, like polite conversation, spiritual discourse should avoid money and politics. But Christian spirituality can never accept such artificial boundaries. All they do is protect foolishness – foolish systems, foolish people, and foolish behavior. So, let's see if we can discern the path of wisdom in the marketplace.

The Story of Consumerism

Humans have been consuming things as long as we have existed. But, for millennia, that consumption was limited to food and things needed for survival. Fast forward to the present and the mayhem associated with Black Fridays where we now see normally reasonable adults who are prepared to throw punches over discounted TVs! How did we ever get to this point?

The answer is that it didn't happen by chance. It was the result of the sophisticated engineering of desire that began early in the twentieth century when, as one commentator describes it, "the advertising industry began to use psychological techniques to pour gasoline onto the flames of yearning."[150] The march toward a consumer society went into high gear after World War 2 when business and governments were confronted with the need to rebuild the economy.

> The story of consumerism is the story of engineered desire.

Economist and retailing analyst Victor Lebow spelled out the shocking way to address this challenge:

Our enormously productive economy . . . demands that we make consumption our way of life, that we convert the buying and use of goods into rituals, that we seek our spiritual satisfaction, our

> ego satisfaction, in consumption . . . we need things consumed,
> burned up, replaced and discarded at an ever-accelerating rate.[151]

Looking back, it is clear that his plan was adopted and that it has worked just as he envisaged. And if that doesn't disturb you, let me tell you why I think it should.

In the years since Lebow articulated the proposal for economic recovery, the developed world has become little more than a collection of consumer societies. The primary identity of members of these societies has become that of consumer and the primary way that our value is measured and demonstrated is by how much and what we consume.

The full story of consumerism requires placing consumption into the larger context of the materials economy. However, since others tell that larger story well[152] I will limit myself to a few comments on the dark sides of natural resource extraction, manufacturing, and the excessive consumption of the products we have learned to love and need.

The Depletion of Natural Resources

The story starts with extraction of raw materials from the earth since they form part of all the stuff we consume. This includes the things we mine, farm, harvest from the oceans, or reap in any other way – many of those ways, of course, being better described as rape or plunder. The reason this strong language is appropriate is the massive level of over-extraction that has been taking place during recent years.

The Global Footprint Network has been tracking the gap between human demand on nature (ecological footprint) and nature's capacity to meet that demand (biological capacity) for nearly 150 countries since 1961.[153]

In 1961, we were extracting 73% of the global biological capacity for raw materials and were, therefore, living within our means. However, each year since then, population growth and increasing consumption put more pressure on earth's ecosystems. This has resulted in such things as water shortages, reduced cropland productivity, deforestation, biodiversity loss, fisheries collapse and climate change.

> In the last 30 years alone we have extracted one third of the planet's total natural resources.

By 1970 we were extracting 100% of the global biological capacity each year, and of course, that capacity was reducing every year. Every year since then we have been taking more out of the earth than it is capable of reproducing. By 2000 that over-extraction reached 187% and levels of extraction have increased annually since then, as have, correspondingly, the levels of biocapacity. Picture the graphic representation of this – increasing extraction from ever decreasing reserves.[154]

In the last 30 years alone we have extracted one third of the planet's total natural resources.[155] Every year we mine 55 billion tons of bio-mass, fossil energy, metal and minerals from the earth. This is almost

10 tons for every person in the world – and obviously people in the west consume a disproportionally high share of this.[156]

If earth's history is compressed to one calendar year, we humans have existed for only 23 minutes but within that time we have used 33% of earth's natural resources within the last 0.2 seconds.[157]

75% of global fisheries now are fished at or beyond capacity.[158] 80% of the planet's original forests are gone.[159] In the Amazon alone, we are losing 2000 trees a minute.[160] It's hard to call this anything other than foolishly reckless plunder. And what drove all of this? The answer is simple – consumer demand for more stuff.

Clearly we are running out of the natural resources needed to provide us with the food and things we have come to need or want. But worse, we have been destroying the earth in doing so. The crisis isn't that we are fast approaching exhausted global supplies of such things as the rare earth elements needed to run our cell phones but that earth has been raped and seriously damaged by our obsession with consuming stuff.

The Dark Side of Manufacturing

Manufacturing also reveals similar patterns of foolishness. Ever-accelerating rates of consumption and disposal of our consumables are, as we saw in the astounding quote from retailing analyst Victor Lebow, also skilfully engineered. Recall his shocking admission that the economy demands that things be "consumed, burned up, replaced and discarded at an ever-accelerating rate."[161]

Planned obsolescence – both actual and perceived – are the key tools that manipulate us into doing our part to maintain the consumer system. The things we have been manipulated into loving and needing are designed for the dump.[162] The trick is how to keep us content with shorter and shorter life spans of our consumables.

Actual obsolescence is when things are designed to malfunction and no longer be usable. But, since things cannot break fast enough to maintain the engines of commerce, perceived obsolescence ups the game by making us willing to throw away products that are still working perfectly well simply to get their new, updated versions. If the picture isn't becoming clear as to how this works, think cell phones and other digital devices.

But, of course, planned obsolescence is not limited to electronics. The fashion industry is perhaps an even better example. According to Vanessa Friedman, the driving force of fashion is planned obsolescence.[163] Sustainable fashion is an oxymoron. Everything in fashion is designed to lead consumers to abandon the old and embrace the new. Fashion is the golden girl in marketing circles because she leads the way toward shorter and shorter cycles of perceived obsolescence and leaves fashion aficionados anxiously anticipating rather than begrudging the next cycle of new purchases.

Another dark side of manufacturing our consumables is that the real costs are hidden and, more importantly, never passed on to the consumer. For example, the energy required to manufacture an IPhone is 73 times greater than the energy required to charge it for one year of continuous use.[164] Many environmentalists agree that the energy involved in making the stuff we buy is the major way that we contribute to environmental problems – more major than even the natural resource extraction.[165]

But the energy costs of manufacturing are by far not the only hidden costs. Even more serious are the human costs associated with all the underpaid and often exploited people who provide the required labor for the manufacturing process.

In Bangladesh, for example, where approximately five thousand readymade garment factories generate 80% of the country's exports to the West, the average labor rate for these workers in these factories is $0.31 USD per hour.[166] Even after catastrophic events like the collapse of the Rana Plaza garment factory in 2013, which killed 1,136 people, little has changed because suppliers have little bargaining power because they are competing against suppliers in other low-income nations. It's the proverbial race to the bottom.[167] And clearly we are not the ones paying the hidden costs of our consumables.

Change is Possible

The story of the rise and excesses of consumerism is a discouraging one. But there are things we can do about it and there are alternative strategies being offered to make the materials economy more sustainable. Examples of these include movements and organizations such as Green Chemistry[168] (protecting the environment by inventing new chemical processes that do not pollute), Zero Waste[169] (following the pattern of natural cycles, where all waste is recovered and put to use by others), and Renewable Energy[170] (switching from dependence on fossil fuels to things like wind, solar, tidal, geothermal power). But there are also things we can do as individuals.

Think of the 3 R's of sustainability – reduce, reuse, and recycle. Let me deal with them in the reverse order, starting with recycling which is the easiest to do and great place to start.

Recycling is important and definitely worth doing, particularly the recycling of aluminum, paper and cardboard.[171] The combined effects of recycling and composting prevented the release of approximately 186 million metric tons of carbon dioxide in 2013, comparable to taking over 39 million cars off the road for a year.[172] So it does make a difference.

However, while recycling is a good start, it is a bad place to stop. There are at least two reasons why it will never be enough. First, household waste is just the tip of the iceberg. For every one garbage can of waste you put out on the curb, 70 garbage cans of waste were made upstream just to make the junk in that one garbage can you put out on the curb.[173] Additionally, it is impossible to recycle much of our garbage because it contains too many toxics or, by design, was never intended to be recyclable. We need to do more than recycle. We need to reduce consumption.

Reusing is preferable to recycling because it does not involve any processing costs. One of the easiest ways to reduce consumption is by delaying replacement of products until they are no longer either working or repairable. Repairing things is often much more difficult than replacing them. After one of our downsizings, my wife and I decided to pay to have a favourite sofa rebuilt to fit our new condo. Finding someone to do the work was not easy and our cost was about the same as purchasing a new one. But we had the immense satisfaction of taking a small step toward a sustainable lifestyle.

Reusing is, of course, a way of **reducing** consumption. Sharing is another way doing the same. This will be a familiar pattern to many of us who have practiced sharing goods and services with friends. What's new in the sharing economy is finding ways to do this with strangers, and to do it in order to make money. Airbnb and Uber are two well-established examples of this new emerging trend and many others are springing up daily.

Sharing reduces consumption by reducing private ownership. No longer limited to housing and cars, sharing, renting and exchanging enterprises are now springing up for sharing clothing, electronics, small appliances, tools, baby toys, and much more. While still in the early days of their development there is definitely potential in these sharing strategies that will, from a retail point of view of, understandably be seen as subversive.

Another commercial form of sharing this has been rapidly developing in larger urban settings is bartering systems where goods and services are exchanged instead of currency.[174] Bartering is, of course, a much older system of exchange than currency exchange, and it is being rediscovered by millennials who want to avoid or minimize ownership but need access to things which, when they no longer need them, they can pass on to someone else.

> Live simply so that others may simply live.

Some people will say that these strategies to reduce consumption and make life more sustainably are overly idealistic. I stand with Annie Leonard who responds to this charge by saying that those who believe that we can continue to do what we have been doing are the ones who are idealistic.[175] That is the truly unrealistic option!

Living Simply

Another way of describing these ways of intentional reducing consumption is living simply. Simple living is not a new idea. It has deep roots in both the Old and New Testaments. As Augur prayed in the book of Proverbs, "Don't let me be too poor or too rich. Give me just what I need."[176] In the same way, the teachings of Jesus contained constant warnings against the dangers of riches, which he argued, led to hardness of the heart to other people and deadness of the heart in relation to God

By both his life and his words Jesus taught voluntary simplicity – what Millennials today call, minimalism. This has always been the cornerstone of Christian monasticism. We also see living simply as a central practice in a number of Christian traditions. One good example is The Friends (also known as Quakers) who have long made simple living their most fundamental spiritual practice. They take Mahatma Gandhi's mantra as their own - "Live simply so that others may simply live."

This reminds us that the motive of simply living is not asceticism but compassion. It is this heart-posture that makes simple living such a deeply Christian practice. Recall Jesus' words, "The one who has two shirts must share with someone who has none, and the one who has food must do the same."[177] These are not easy words to hear but they reflect the subversive spirit of Jesus that we so easily miss when we choose to worship him rather than follow him.

Simple living requires detachment – not, first and foremost, from our possessions but from our identities as consumers. It requires letting go of our investment in images that require the bolstering of excess consumption. It requires no longer relying on retail therapy for the alleviation of our boredom or stress. It requires living with softened and lessened attachments to all the external things that we use to pump up our otherwise vulnerable egos.

Christians sometimes think of detachment as a Buddhist virtue, failing to realize how deeply Christian both the concept and practice are. Jesus taught and lived non-attachment. Think, for example, of his teaching about the impossibility of loving both God and money,[178] his warning of the danger of attachment to material possessions,[179] even one's family.[180] If you didn't know better, Jesus could easily be confused with a Buddhist monk!

Detachment is not indifference or a wilful, teeth-clenching refusal to enjoy what is good and beautiful. It is primarily an action of the heart. Detachment involves loosening our grasp on the physical, psychological and spiritual things that reinforce our fundamental orientation toward possessiveness. We detach so our attachments can be re-ordered and re-aligned. Then, cooperating with the inflow of Grace to our deepest self, we can allow love to pass through us to touch and heal others and the world.

Detachment makes it possible for us to passionately and creatively engage with God's transformational work in the world. Far from passivity, detachment prepares us for true action as opposed to simple reaction. It prepares us for full participation in God's cosmic plan of making all things new and whole in and through Christ. It prepares us to be the incarnation of Wisdom that we are called to be.

Pausing
to Ponder

1. This chapter has given you a lot of information. But, hopefully it has also given you a chance to reflect on your lifestyle, patterns of consumerism, and ways of relating to your possessions and money. What did you find most challenging or shocking in what you have read? What invitations to live differently did you experience? How do you plan on responding to those invitations?

2. How could you live more simply so that others could simply live? What first steps in that direction could you start with today, or if not today, this week?

Additional Readings and Things to Ponder

The Internet provides an enormous range of resources to help you reflect further on the issues raised in this chapter and begin to live with more wisdom and less foolishness. If you haven't done so already, go back through the chapter and look at the references as they contain many websites and other possible places to take these things further.

One of the references is to the YouTube video, *The Story of* Stuff. It presents an excellent overview of the story of excess consumption. Find it at https://www.youtube.com/watch?v=9GorqroigqM then, after watching it, get some friends together and watch it again. Then take some time to talk together about what you as a group can do to respond to the issues it raises. After viewing it, you might also be interested to see the many shorter, follow-up videos that have been produced by the same people and give the detailed story of the important overlooked issues associated with such things as bottled water, cosmetics, electronics and many other consumables. You will find on the same YouTube link to *The Story of Stuff.*

21   Living Compassion

As we are beginning to see, wisdom either flows through daily life, affecting everything we do or it isn't worthy of being called wisdom.

But how can we know if we are living our lives wisely or foolishly? The hallmark of wisdom is not how you deal with any one of the illustrative issues we have been considering in this section. How much you recycle, reduce or reuse consumables is not the most important criterion of whether or not you are living wisely. Nor is whether or not you identify with nature or spend regular time in it.

> The measure of wisdom is not so much *what* you do but *how* and *why* you do it.

The single most important measure of living wisdom is not so much *what* you do as *how* and *why* you do it. What you do is important, but how and why you do it are crucial. If love guides your actions to care for the earth and other people, then the chances are good you are living wisely.

Wisdom and Love

Wisdom and love are intimately interwoven. In the absence of love, wisdom is more apparent than real. And love that is not expressed with wisdom is not authentic love.

How could it be otherwise? The Spirit of Wisdom that inhabits everything that exists is the Spirit of God. Wisdom flows from its source in the Godhead as manifest love. You simply cannot have wisdom apart from love.

While it is common to speak of God as love, Cynthia Bourgeault suggests that the reason we can say this of God is because God loves. A quality of being such as love cannot be known apart from being manifest. God has the quality of love because God enacts love.[181] And the same is true of wisdom. Both have to be lived to be real. They have to be manifest to be anything more than an abstraction.

Love is the deeply personal presence of the Spirit of Wisdom at the heart of the universe and at the heart of its continuing evolution. It is the fire that breathes life into matter. It is the force that holds all things together and draws them forward toward wholeness and fullness in Christ. Drawing together and whole-making is the nature of love because it is the nature of the Spirit of Wisdom, the Spirit of God.

The First Manifestation commonly described as the Big Bang was an outflow of Love and Wisdom. This is why Love and Wisdom form the warp and woof of the universe. Everything within the universe carries their imprint because it carries the imprint of God. This is why wisdom is so deeply connected to the natural world and why, like anything, wisdom can only be truly known and lived through love that is manifest.

Love changes how we see people and issues. This is why action that emerges from any other motive can so easily be self serving. If you have ever had any involvement with social justice work you probably encountered angry people whose work toward this worthy goal arises out of their anger rather than compassion. What they are doing is important but how they are doing it contaminates their work and soul. As Jesus pointed out so poignantly, what we do and what we say arise from our hearts and it is this heart motivation that is of most importance to God.[182]

Learning to live wisdom involves recognizing and trusting the fact that Wisdom already resides at the core of our being. We are made in the image and likeness of God and we retain the imprint of love and wisdom that is our birthright. But, as we have seen, we can only access wisdom through the awakening of our hearts that allows us to see people and issues through the eyes of Christ.

> The source of our inner light and compassion is God's indwelling presence.

When I see through those eyes of Christ-in-me and me-in-Christ, I cannot help but love and have compassion for everything and everyone I see. This is because what and who I am actually seeing is God's indwelling presence in the world.[183] God's indwelling presence in me becomes my inner light that allows me to see God's indwelling presence in everyone and everything that exists.

This inner light is also he source of the compassion we are asked to pass on to others. And it is the source of the love we are to share when we love others as ourselves.[184]

Loving others as ourselves leads to compassionate engagement with those we encounter. It isn't enough to simply *feel* compassion. If it is to be an authentic expression of wisdom our compassion must be lead to some form of active engagement. Obviously we cannot be engaged with everyone we encounter. What's important is that we notice the compassion that arises in our hearts and respond to it in some way.

Moved by Compassion

Compassion is often confused with empathy. While they are related, they are quite different.

Empathy involves the sense of knowing what the other person is experiencing. If, for example, the other person is suffering, you also experience suffering and, because you identify with them, you assume that their suffering has become yours. But, your identification with the other person makes it easy for you to lose sight of the fact that what you are feeling is simply your *response* to them, not actually their experience. Without being clear about this distinction it is easy for empathy to become overwhelming – even crippling.

Compassion requires a basic capacity for empathy but is not based on identification. It starts with an inner posture of compassionate openness to the other person that allows us to come alongside them without losing sight of the fact that we are not them and they are not us. When we respond from a place of empathic identification with someone who is suffering we feel *for* them whereas when we respond from compassion we feel *with* them. But the biggest difference is that instead of simply feeling badly for them, compassion leads us to do something for them.

> ## Compassion moves us to respond, not simply feel.

Compassion moves us to respond, not simply feel. It moves us toward some form of active engagement.

Both Jesus' teaching and life richly illustrate this responsive dimension of compassion. So often the Gospels speak of Jesus being moved by compassion.

Think of his response to the man with leprosy who came to Jesus on his knees, begging:

> If you are willing, you can make me clean.
> Moved with compassion, Jesus reached out his hand and
> touched him.
> I am willing, he said. Be made clean.[185]

Or, think of the day when, on his way to the town called Nain, Jesus encountered a dead man being carried out of the town for burial. Seeing his mother and knowing that this was her only son, Jesus was again moved with compassion and brought her son back to life.[186]

We encounter the same dynamic of compassion leading to engagement in the story of his healing of the two blind men,[187] the feeding of large crowds of people who came to hear him speak,[188] and his healing of the sick when they tracked him down and intruded in his time for much needed solitude.[189]

Compassion is also the heart of what is perhaps his most famous story – the story of the Good Samaritan.[190] After being ignored and passed by a priest and a priest's assistant, a Samaritan came upon a Jew who had been left half dead after a robbery. Moved by compassion, he bandaged his wounds, sat him on his own animal, brought him to an inn, and took care of him. This is compassion in action.

Compassion goes beyond trying to alleviate suffering. It impels us to also work tirelessly to prevent it. This starts, in the words of Jesus, with treating others as we wish to be treated by them.[191] But don't think of this simply as common decency. It is much more than this. Reframing the Golden Rule (Matthew 7: 12) in terms of the Great Commandment (Mark 12: 28-34) helps us see how radical this foundation of compassion really is. What it asks of us is that we treat others as ourselves.[192] When self-interest is broadened to include all others it means working to ensure that they receive the fairness and justice we wish for ourselves.

This is the point where compassion flows into social justice. How can it do anything less if we affirm the wisdom of the Great Commandment?

The truth is that we are responsible for our brothers and sisters – not simply, our brothers and sisters within our family or faith tradition but our brothers and sisters in the human family.

Seen through the mind and heart of Christ we begin to experience kinship with all of creation. It will always, of course, be easiest to experience solidarity with other humans since the image of God is most clearly discerned in them. This is why, when asked how she could spend her life serving the poorest of the poor on the streets of Calcutta, Mother Teresa answered that in every face she saw Jesus. She described it as, "Seeing and adoring the presence of Jesus in the distressing disguise of the poor."[193]

> How did we ever come to think that worshiping God while ignoring his commandments was an option?

This is what Jesus meant when he said that what we do to others we do to him.[194]

It is quite alarming to see the way in which Christians disregard the example of Jesus and clear teaching of Scriptures to defend the rights of the poor[195] and to work for justice for the oppressed and persecuted.[196] How did we ever come to think that worshipping God while ignoring his commandments was an option?

A biblical view of social justice does not require a redistribution of resources. Our responsibility is much simpler and more realistic: to care for the oppressed and seek to stop others from oppressing them; to speak up for those who are being persecuted; and to work for laws that protect all peoples regardless of race, nationality, economic status, or political or religious affiliation.[197]

This is not a radical ideology of liberal Christianity. Working toward not just the alleviation of the suffering of individuals but changing the systems that perpetuate suffering and oppression should be the mission of all those who follow Christ.

Living compassion is following the wisdom of the heart and mind of Christ. A life without the compassion of Christ flowing through it is a life that can never truly transcend self-interest. It is, therefore, foolishness.

Pausing to Ponder

1. *In this chapter I suggested that the hallmark of wisdom is love. Self-deception being what it is, we can, of course, still easily fool ourselves about our true motivation. But, love that flows into action can reflect wisdom whereas the absence of love means the absence of wisdom. Take a few moments to reflect on the place love plays in your acts of compassion* – and on the way in which your compassion leads to active engagement with those who suffer.

2. *Compassion goes beyond trying to alleviate suffering. It impels us to work tirelessly to prevent it. In this chapter I suggest that this is the point where compassion flows into social justice. How do you exercise your responsibility for your brothers and sisters - not simply in the faith but in the human family ~ particularly those who you read and hear about but will likely never meet?*

Additional Readings and Things to Ponder

Three books that will help you live with the compassionate heart of Christ:

- Andrew Dreitcer, *Living Compassion: Loving Like Jesus* (Upper Room, 2017)

- Karen Armstrong, *Twelve Steps to a Compassionate Life* (Anchor, 2011)

- Timothy Keller, *Generous Justice: How God's Grace Makes us Just* (New York, NY: Penguin Books, 2012)

22   Wisdom as Choice and Lifestyle

Wisdom involves a choice between two paths. It is a choice that must be made over and over again until eventually it becomes a lifestyle. But one or the other of these paths will eventually become your lifestyle.

The path of foolishness is the path walked by the vast majority of people who simply think they are living their lives in the way everyone knows is how you live life.

The rules for living they are following are the implicit ones of their culture. Culture is much more important in shaping how we see and live than most people recognize and its role in spirituality has generally been overlooked. What culture teaches us forms the foundation of how we understand and relate to life. Often this is deeply incongruent with the values and views encouraged by our religious traditions, but the process of enculturation is so subtle and powerful that we usually fail to recognize the deepest of these pernicious forms of foolishness.

Within Christianity, the so-called prosperity gospel is a good example of accommodation to culture. But, it is quite easy to identify many others. Typically, however, we miss the most serious accommodations while focusing on ones that tend to be little more than distractions. At the risk of oversimplification, conservatives, for example, often focus on things like sexuality and teaching of evolution in schools while liberals often focus on implementing agendas of political correctness.

However, much more basic than any of these is accommodation to the cultural myth of the separate self and a desacralized cosmos. When earth is no longer sacred, nothing is sacred. Once nature is an "it," everything and everyone else easily becomes an "it" – separate from us. Rather than recognizing creation as a sacred manifestation of the Divine we think of it as simply a resource that exists for us. It belongs to us; we don't belong to it.

Is it any wonder we feel alone? Is it any wonder that our default response to life is to grasp and possess all we can and do everything possible to ignore the consequences of this to others and to the world itself? Is it any wonder that the pursuit of power and personal happiness is the unquestioned rule of life?

The path to wisdom is dramatically different. On this path we know that, like us, nature is a manifestation of God. This means that we are a part of nature and part of everything that exists. Knowing this allows us to live with a fundamental sense of belonging. We know our place within the enchanted web of life. And with this, we know our responsibility to care for everyone and everything else that is also a manifestation of God.

As members of one body, the body of Christ, we know the inherent dignity and worth of all other parts of the body. We know that, "If one member suffers, all the members suffer with it."[198] This is why we are moved by compassion for the needs of all who are a part of this same living body of Christ within which everything that exists belongs.

It is this solidarity with everything in existence – particularly with the earth – that makes it possible for us to escape the treadmill of excessive consumerism. Doing so will not be easy as it runs against the surging current of our consumer culture. But it is possible.

Getting off the treadmill of excessive consumerism does not mean that we will no longer buy things. It simply means that we will no longer use possessions as the basis of our identity and as a way of bolstering our sense of worth and importance.

Like Neo in the movie, *The Matrix*, who chooses to exit the dream world and walk out into reality, everything changes when we begin to recognize the sacredness of everything in existence and the preciousness of all life. When we do, we begin see that *how* we live has an effect on everything and everyone. Rather than being isolated selves we know that we are all part of the body of God. And once we recognize this, we begin to relate to everything beyond us as a "Thou" – another part in the larger whole that is God. Now we have found our true and deepest places of belonging.

This is real belonging – not the superficial attachment of those who share beliefs or spiritual tribes but the profound belonging that comes from being part of the same body[199], branches of the same vine.[200]

With that belonging come responsibilities. Self-interest with episodic expression of love for others is no longer enough. Loving others as ourselves becomes the foundation of our compassion and we move out into the world with caring, informed ways of repairing and preserving the planet. With eyes that now see, we align ourselves with what God is doing in the world to make all things new and whole in Christ. This is the path of living wisdom.

Seeing, Knowing, and Acting

Choices become patterns as they are repeated over and over again. And patterns, when established and lived, consolidate into lifestyles.

Take, for example, choices around what you eat. Suppose junk food has been a major part of your diet for many years. First steps toward healthier eating will be difficult and will require repeated choices of fresh whole foods over fast food. But, over time, these choices will become more automatic. They will become your habitual eating pattern. Eventually, it will become unimaginable for you to eat as you once did. By this point healthy eating will have become a lifestyle.

This is, of course, a smart thing to do because eating junk food is foolish and eating healthy food is smart. But wisdom isn't simply doing smart things. Nor is it the accumulation of many little good decisions. It is much more than healthy eating or even wellness. As we have seen earlier, wisdom flows from awakening and is reinforced by actions you take in response to this.

> The small decisions are the really important ones!

The awakening of our hearts and minds through the acquisition of the heart and mind of Christ is the ground out of which we begin to see what truly is. This is how we come to know our place in God and God's place in us. This is how we come to a deep awareness of the sacredness and interconnectedness of everything in existence. Only then do real choices become possible. And once we see the folly of the path we have been on, choices become easier. But, they must be made, and they must be made over and over again.

Nothing we can do will produce an awakening. It is pure grace – a gift of God. Our part is to notice and then nurture it when we receive it. We do this by acting on what we see and know. Responding to whatever light we have received keeps us awake, fuels our appetite for further learning and growth, and helps us remain open to deeper awakenings and transformation.

This is the journey of our ongoing conversion. It's a journey of many Good Friday deaths and many Easter Sunday resurrections. It's a journey of awakenings, of acting on what we see and know in that awakening, and through this offering our consent to the ongoing transformational work of God in us.

Wise Choices

If the choices we make keep us on a path of either foolishness of wisdom, making good decisions at the many choice points we encounter each day is tremendously important. Discernment is seeing things clearly and then being able to make wise choices. Understood this way it becomes immediately clear that discernment lies right at the heart of living wisdom.

Too often Christians think of discernment in narrowly religious terms. They might speak of discerning a religious calling, or attempting to discern God's will around who to marry or which of several jobs to take. But while we all face important decisions from time to time, choices abound every minute of every hour of every day. And discernment is at least as relevant in helping us make wise small choices as it is in making wise big decisions.

In fact, I'd say that the small decisions are the really important ones. Once we begin to regularly live with wisdom and discernment in relation to the small daily matters, the big decisions tend to follow the patterns already established and are often quite easily made.

Although the mind has a significant role to play in discernment, the role of the heart is even more important. I understand why you might find this surprising. So let me give you a quick introduction to what I take to be the genius of the understanding of discernment that was developed by the sixteenth century giant of Christian spirituality, St. Ignatius of Loyola.

Alignment and Misalignment

The starting point of discernment is recognizing our fundamental heart orientation. As we noted earlier, habits of the heart provide the organizing threads of our lives. The more deeply these habits are integrated and aligned with each other the more they also serve as what I would call our fundamental heart or life orientation.

Since you have read this far in this book, I am going to assume that your heart, like mine, is basically directed toward God. This does not mean that you are always true to this fundamental life orientation. Competing loves likely creep back in as countercurrents that add turbulence and complicate your floating in the river that is God. But I suspect that it is highly unlikely that you would choose to now change direction and follow any of those crosscurrents as your new life direction.

Discernment begins by noticing your inner experience when you are in the flow of your heart orientation – that is, open to and in sync with God, no distractions, no resistance, just at one within yourself and with the river of God in which you flow. Let's call this alignment.

Now contrast this to your inner experience when you are caught up in the turbulence of the cross currents of your life – when you are out of alignment with God and with your deepest self. Pay close attention to the experience of misalignment because the difference between these two sets of inner experience will be at the core of how you will make wise choices.

St. Ignatius was vastly ahead of his time. The way he suggests we make those wise choices anticipated the best understandings of the psychospiritual dynamics of the soul that four centuries later we now have. But, to make his suggestion practical, let me first set the context with some illustrative choice points we will face if we are trying to live with wisdom:

- Whether to buy the inexpensive, but toxic, household cleaner or the more expensive non-toxic one
- Whether to replace or repair a used car, and if you decide to replace it, what choice would best honor the sacred nature of earth

⚜ Whether to buy sustainable fish or ignore this added complexity to your shopping decisions

⚜ Whether to buy bottled water

⚜ Whether to invest in companies with an ecological conscience or simply go with the hope of the largest return on investment.

We face choices like these all the time, regardless of whether or not we are aware of them. So, how are we to make a wise decision once we become aware that that we are facing one of them?

In somewhat simplified terms that I think are good enough for us at the moment, St. Ignatius would suggest a two step process of decision making.

> Discernment is calibrating your inner compass.

The first step is to engage the mind by reading as much as is possible and helpful in thinking about the issues. Then, write out a list of pros and cons of acting in each of the ways that are suggested by the situation. Consider also any direct Biblical wisdom that seems pertinent. And then ponder all these considerations in your mind for a period of time.

Avoid rushing to a decision. Think carefully, talk with trusted others about the decision and the things you have come to feel are worthy considerations in support of one action or another. But take your time. That's what it means to ponder with your mind.

The next step is to ponder the matter in your heart. The starting place in this process is to set a period of time that you can give to this stage of the process – the more important the decision, the longer the time you should set aside for discernment. Then divide that time in half and for the first half assume that you are going to take whichever decision your mind was leading you to. Live this decision as fully as you can, no longer thinking about it, just noticing what arises in your spirit and soul as you assume that this will be the decision you will make. Then, with the remaining half of the time, do the opposite. Assume you will take the opposite decision. And once again, notice what arises in your heart.

Notice the difference in your inner experience between when you were assuming you would make one decision versus the other. Being as honest as you can, notice which one carries with it that sense of alignment that I talked about. And which carries with it much more the sense of mis-alignment?

I have been prayerfully using this as the framework for both my moment-by-moment decisions and the bigger ones for the last 25 years. Of course, there are times when I choose not to engage this powerful spiritual discernment tool but when I don't it is because I have already made my decision and I simply do not want to be confronted with its folly. However, this simple exercise has been singularly helpful to me over those years, and to nearly everyone I have ever introduced to it.

It's a way of calibrating and learning to trust your inner compass. Of course that process is highly subjective. But how could anyone expect decision making to be anything other than subjective. Opening your Bible at random and pointing a blind finger at some verse is equally subjective but it is also highly irrational. And yet I hear of Christians who practice this sort of superstitious behavior.

Short of an email, text message or phone call from God, I can think of no possible way in which we can experience divine guidance that is not subjective. But this way of St. Ignatius grounds discernment in both heart and head and has stood the test of time. It is a rich part of our Christian spiritual heritage, even if you have never heard of it before.

Living Wisdom

Don't settle for making one-by-one decisions. Allow wisdom to become so deeply your lifestyle that your single choice is to live in deep alignment with God and with God's cosmic agenda of God making all things new and whole in Christ. You will be amazed how much falls in place when you do – how simple life becomes and how incredibly satisfying it is to float in the river of life that is God. Just keep paying attention to the inner compass of your heart. If you do, it will let you know quite clearly when you are out of alignment.

The wisest people I know still face daily decisions but they tell me that those decisions are generally quite easy. It is only a matter of whether they go with the flow of God in them and in the world or, for a moment or two, step out of that flow in order to purse some pleasure or gratification that they know is unwise.

Don't expect perfection in walking the wisdom path. Just be sure you notice when you have wandered off the path and get back on it as soon as possible. Doing so requires that you attend to your heart and reinforces your fundamental life direction. Not attending to your heart is to take the default path of foolishness.

Choose wisdom. Doing so is choosing God.

Pausing to Ponder

1. *Being as honest as you can, which of the two paths – wisdom and foolishness – has characterized most of your life to this point? What has kept you from fully embracing a life of wisdom?*

2. *What has blocked you from responding with more consent to the invitations you have been receiving?*

3. *What has been your discernment process when faced with important decisions? How do you react to the discernment process described in this chapter and drawn from the Ignatian spiritual tradition? What important decisions do you currently face and how do you plan to approach them?*

Additional Readings and Things to Ponder

For a much fuller discussion of discernment and its role in the purification of desires and realignment of the will see, David G. Benner,

Desiring God's Will: Aligning Our Heart with the Heart of God –
Expanded Edition (Downers Grove, IVP Books, 2015).

For a wonderful discussion of how to learn to attune and trust your inner
compass written from the perspective of Ignatian Spirituality, see
Margaret Silf, *Inner Compass: An Invitation to Ignatian Spirituality*
(Chicago: Loyola Press, 1999).

About the Author

Dr. David G. Benner is the Founding Director of *CASCADIA – A LIVING WISDOM COMMUNITY*. He is an internationally known depth psychologist, author, and wisdom teacher whose life's work has been directed toward facilitating not merely healing or even growth, but the unfolding of the self associated with a journey of awakening and transformation.

David has authored or edited more than 30 books that have been translated into 24 foreign languages. He has held faculty appointments at numerous universities, colleges and seminaries in North America; served as Chief or Senior Psychologist in a number of clinics and hospitals in Canada and USA, and as Consulting Psychologist throughout South America, South East Asia, Scandinavia, Australia, New Zealand, and Southern Africa; and has lectured and led workshops and retreats in more than 30 countries around the world.

David's citations and honours include being named in *International Men of Achievement*, *The Directory of Distinguished Americans*, *The International Book of Honour*, *Dictionary of International Biography*, *International Directory of Distinguished Leadership*, *Who's Who Among Human Service Professionals*, and *Who's Who in Theology and Science*.

Beyond his work in psychology, spirituality and wisdom teaching his other principal interests are walking, sailing, cycling, jazz, good food and soulful conversation. David and his wife, Juliet Benner – author of *Contemplative Vision: A Guide to Christian Art and Prayer*, live in Toronto, Canada.

CASCADIA – A Living Wisdom Community

Cascadia is an online, intentionally small group of people who seek to learn and grow together as we live the wisdom and compassion that flows from an awakened heart and transformed consciousness.

From the outside *Cascadia* could appear to be a school since we have mentors and teachers, suggested readings that we discuss, and inner and outer practices that we teach and learn. But from the inside it feels more like a learning community that is built around sharing the journey of awakening and transformation, and supporting each other as we attempt to live with wisdom and compassion.

While many of us find our home base in the Christian wisdom tradition, this does not mean that we teach Christian beliefs or that members have to believe anything in particular. The Christian wisdom tradition is not a set of beliefs to be embraced but a transformational path to be walked. Beyond the Christian tradition we also draw on many other sources of wisdom, including the wisdom of the Perennial tradition, other faiths and spiritual traditions, Indigenous spirituality, depth psychology, body wisdom, cosmology, and eco-spirituality.

Interested in learning more about us?
Send an email to Cascadia.LiveWisdom@gmail.com.

Endnotes

[1] New Jerusalem Bible. Unless otherwise specified, all Scripture references are from the Christian Standard Bible (CSB).

[2] Luke 2: 19.

[3] This is my own loose rendering of these verses.

[4] 1 Kings 4: 29-34.

[5] 1 Kings 11: 1-10.

[6] C. G. Jung, *Letters, Vol. 2: 1951-1961*, Gerhard Adler, ed. (Princeton, NJ: Princeton University Press, 1976), pp. 579-580.

[7] 2 Chronicles 1: 7-12.

[8] https://thebulletin.org/2018-doomsday-clock-statement

[9] https://academic.oup.com/bioscience/advance-article/doi/10.1093/biosci/bix125/4605229

[10] Romans 8: 20–22.

[11] Words drawn from a prayer of St. Francis of Assisi, *The Canticle of the Creatures*, found at http://prayerfoundation.org/canticle_of_brother_sun.htm

[12] My thanks to Fr. Martin Brokenleg for helping me understand the make-up of a family in Lakota culture. I, however, remain responsible for any errors in this rendering.

[13] http://www.wolfwalkercollection.com/articles/aho-mitakuye-oyasin To see the same understanding in a very different cultural context, you might want to watch a short YouTube video of Uncle Bob Randall, an elder of Yankunytjatjara people of Uluru (Ayer's Rock) in central Australia, explaining what knowing the sacred interconnectedness of

everything in existence means to him and his people. Find it at www.youtube.com/watch?v=w0sWIVR1hXw&feature=youtu.be

[14] The film, *Aluna*, is still widely available. In many parts of the world if can be accessed on Netflix or YouTube, in others it can be downloaded free of charge or for a nominal rental, and in yet others it can be purchased through Amazon. Details about its availability in your region can be found at http://www.alunathemovie.com/

[15] My knowledge of the Kogi comes from my son, Sean Benner, who, at the invitation of the Kogi, made this hike to help the Kogi develop their tourism-as-education project for Younger Brother.

[16] Max Born, *The Born-Einstein Letters* (London, UK: The Macmillan Press, 1971), p. 155.

[17] Colossians 1: 15 – 17; 1 Corinthians 12: 12 – 30.

[18] Rupert Sheldrake, A New Science of Life: The Hypothesis of Formative Causation (Los Angeles, CA: J P Tarcher, 1982).

[19] R. S. Bobrow, "Evidence for a Communal Consciousness," *Explore*, 2011, July-August 7(4), 246-248.

[20] This comment was made by Lulu Miller in a 2015 NPR audio podcast on the science of interconnectedness. Find it at www.npr.org/programs/invisibilia/382451600/entanglement

[21] Although the concept of homeostasis was already present in the scientific physiology literature of the early twentieth century, the first popular account of it and the body wisdom it represented was published by Walter D. Cannon in his book, *The Wisdom of the Body* (New York, NY: W. W. Norton & Company, 1932).

[22] Sigmund Freud, *The Interpretation of Dreams* (New York, NY: Basic Books, 1899/2010).

[23] Wilhelm Reich, *Character Analysis* (New York, NY: Farrar, Straus and Giroux, 1933/1969).

[24] Anna Freud, *The Ego and the Mechanisms of Defense* (London, UK: Routledge, 1992).

[25] http://www.primaltherapy.com/what-is-primal-therapy.php

[26] https://www.psychologytoday.com/ca/therapy-types/gestalt-therapy

[27] http://www.bioenergetic-therapy.com/index.php/en/

[28] www.americanbowen.academy/about-american-bowen-academy/about-bowenwork

[29] https://en.wikipedia.org/wiki/Rolfing

[30] https://alexandertechnique.com/

[31] https://en.wikipedia.org/wiki/Trager_approach

[32] Anodea Judith, *Eastern Body, Western Mind* (New York, NY: Celestial Arts, 2004), p. ix.

[33] Image by LordtNis [CC BY-SA 4.0 (https://creativecommons.org/licenses/by-sa/4.0)], from Wikimedia Commons.

[34] Judith, *ibid*, p. 14.

[35] David G. Benner, *Spirituality and the Awakening Self: The Sacred Journey of Transformation* (Grand Rapids, MI: Brazos Press, 2012).

[36] James Gollnick, "Dream interpretation in the psychology of religion," *Studies in Religion* (Vol 28, Issue 3, 1999) pp. 293-305.

[37] As I describe in more detail in *Spirituality and the Awakening Self, ibid*, dreams serve at least five important psychological functions, all of which involve the unconscious. They express inner experience that is otherwise outside awareness, contribute to the healing of psychic wounds, represent an unconscious effort to creatively generate meaning and coherence to experience, compensate for imbalances of conscious personality, point to lost parts of personality that need to be reclaimed if we are to be whole. This does not include the spiritual and communal functions that traditional and Indigenous cultures recognize

but which depth psychology, with its highly individualistic orientation, still fails to understand.

[38] https://www.huffingtonpost.ca/entry/science-vivid-dreams-religion_us_56e71508e4b0b25c9182de24

[39] *Ibid*. For more on this, see Kelley Bulkeley, *Big Dreams: The Science of Dreaming and the Origins of Religion* (Oxford, UK: Oxford University Press, 2016).

[40] What follows is adapted from, David G. Benner, "Ancient Wisdom for Contemporary Living," *Oneing* (Spring 2013, Vol.1, No. 1), p. 23-28.

[41] Anthony de Mello, *Writings* (Ossining, NY: Orbis, 1999), 15.

[42] Peter N. Borys, Jr., *Transforming Heart and Mind: Learning from the Mystics* (New York: Paulist Press, 2006), 7.

[43] Ephesians 3: 17-19.

[44] By now some of these things should begin to sound familiar since it is the mystics who have contributed the most to the perennial wisdom tradition that we examined in the last chapter.

[45] William Ralph Inge, *Light, Life and Love*, *ibid*, (Kindle Location 156-157).

[46] Barnhart, Bruno, *The Future of Wisdom: Toward a Rebirth of Sapiential Christianity* (Rhinebeck, NY: Monkfish Book Publishing, 2018.)

[47] Cynthia Bourgeault, The Wisdom Jesus: Transforming Heart and Mind – A New Perspective on Christ and His Message (Boston, MA: Shambhala Publications, 2008), p. 23.

[48] Bourgeault, *ibid*, 21.

[49] Barnhart, *ibid*, (Kindle Location 70-71).

[50] Barnhart, *ibid,* (Kindle Location 121).

[51] See, for example, Proverbs 1: 20, 8: 22; Wisdom 6: 17, 22, 7: 24, 9: 9.

[52] Proverbs 8: 22-31, New Jerusalem Bible.

[53] Wisdom 7: 22-28, New Jerusalem Bible.

[54] Proverbs 20: 27.

[55] Proverbs 8: 1-15.

[56] Job 28: 12-19.

[57] Proverbs 8: 11.

[58] Wisdom 6: 12-16, New Jerusalem Bible.

[59] Bruce Sanguin, *Darwin, Divinity and the Dance of the Cosmos* (Kelowna, BC: CopperHouse, 2007), 207.

[60] Sanguin, p. 212. For a more complete review of Biblical scholarship on the relation of Wisdom to God see Elizabeth A. Johnson, *She Who Is* (New York, NY: Crossword Publishing, 1992).

[61] Matthew 11: 19.

[62] Thomas Merton, "Hagia Sophia," in Emblems of a Season of Fury (New York: New Directions, 1963), 66.

[63] Romans 8: 22.

[64] Hafiz, *Somebody Should Start Laughing*: www.101bananas.com/poems/hafiz.html

[65] Proverbs 8: 11.

[66] Erik H. Erikson, *The Life Cycle Completed* (New York, NY: W. W. Norton & Company, 1998).

[67] http://www.nytimes.com/books/99/08/22/specials/erikson-old.html

[68] Richard Rohr, *The Divine Dance: The Trinity and Your Transformation* (New Kensington, PA: Whitaker House, 2016), 61.

[69] Carl McColman, The Big Book of Christian Mysticism: The Essential Guide to Contemplative Spirituality (Charlottesville, VA: Hampton Roads Publishing Company, 2010), 165-166.

[70] New American Standard Version – Anglicsized.

[71] Thomas Merton, *Thoughts in Solitude* (Boston: Shambhala, 1993), 55.

[72] David G. Benner, *Desiring God's Will, Expanded Edition* (Downers Grove, IL: IVP Books, 2015), 77.

[73] For more on the relationship of will and desire as the two major ways of moving forward in the human spiritual journey, see my book, *Desiring God's Will, ibid.*

[74] Mark 10:36.

[75] Wisdom 6: 12 – 16, New Jerusalem Bible.

[76] Marcel Proust, *In Search of Lost Time, Vol. 2: Within a Budding Grove* (New York, NY: Random House, 1998), 596.

[77] See David G. Benner, *Soulful Spirituality: Becoming Fully Alive and Deeply Human* (Grand Rapids, MI: Brazos Press, 2011) for much more on these ways of living soulfully. Also, David G. Benner, *Presence and Encounter: The Sacramental Possibilities of Everyday Life* (Grand Rapids, MI: Brazos Press, 2014).

[78] See David G. Benner, *Human Being and Becoming: Living the Adventure of Life and Love* (Grand Rapids, MI: Brazos Press, 2016) for more on the role of contemplative practices in the awakening of the heart. Also, David G. Benner, *Opening to God: Lectio Divina and Life as Prayer* (Downers Grove, IL: IVP Books, 2010).

[79] See David G. Benner, *Human Being and Becoming, ibid.* for more on this larger perspective of wholeness and its role in transformation and wisdom acquisition.

[80] Proust, *In Search of Lost Time, ibid*, 596-597.

[81] Richard Rohr, https://cac.org/see-everything-judge-little-forgive-much-2017-01-31/

[82] Wisdom 6:16, New Jerusalem Bible.

[83] John 3: 1-5.

[84] Anthony de Mello, *Awakening: Conversations with the Masters* (New York: NY: Image, 2003), 16.

[85] Anthony de Mello, *One Minute Wisdom* (New York: NY: Image, 1988), 11.

[86] Anthony de Mello, *Awareness* (New York: NY: Image, 1992), e-book, 35.

[87] Plato's Allegory of the Cave appeared in his book, *Republic*, written around 380 BC. In this allegory on the nature of reality he distinguished between people who mistake sensory knowledge for the truth and people who really see the truth. A good summary of the allegory and brief discussion of its meaning and significance can be found at https://en.wikipedia.org/wiki/Allegory_of_the_Cave

[88] de Mello, *Awareness,* ibid, 40.

[89] See David G. Benner, *Human Being and Becoming, ibid.* for fuller discussion of the relationship of the heart and mind.

[90] See David G. Benner, *Spirituality and the Awakening Self, ibid.* for a detailed discussion of transformation, including my mapping of the journey of human unfolding.

[91] Barnhart, *ibid,* (Kindle Locations 235-237).

[92] Quoted by Diogenes Allen in an interview with David Cayley broadcast and subsequently published as, *Enlightened by Love: The Thought of Simone Weil* - https://static1.squarespace.com/static/542c2af8e4b00b7cfca08972/t/58ff834a5016e158263f7e09/1493140304361/Enlightened+by+Love.pdf I am thankful to Tom VanGallen for pointing me to this very helpful discussion of the work of Simone Weil, a woman who has an enormous amount to offer any seeker of Wisdom.

[93] Philippians 2: 5.

[94] Acts 2:32, 36.

[95] Richard Rohr, *Loving Both Jesus and Christ*, https://cac.org/loving-jesus-christ-2017-03-31/

[96] Richard Rohr, The Second Coming of Christ, https://cac.org/second-coming-christ-2016-10-30/

[97] Hebrews 1: 3, Jerusalem Bible.

[98] Richard Rohr, *The Christ is Bigger than Christianity* – https://cac.org/christ-bigger-christianity-2017-03-26/

[99] Richard Rohr, *Universal Connection* - https://cac.org/universal-connection-2015-03-27/

[100] Richard Rohr, Loving Both Jesus and Christ, *ibid*.

[101] Thomas Merton, *Thoughts in Solitude* (Boston: Shambhala, 1993), 89.

[102] The *Cloud of Unknowing* is an anonymous work of Christian mysticism written in Middle English in the latter half of the 14th century. It is widely available on the Internet for free download, one of those places being https://www.ccel.org/ccel/anonymous2/cloud

[103] Luke 17: 21.

[104] Matthew 4:17, English Standard Version.

[105] Cynthia Bourgeault, *The Kingdom of Heaven* - https://cac.org/the-kingdom-of-heaven-2017-04-11/

[106] John 18: 36, English Standard Version.

[107] Jim Marion, *Putting on the Mind of Christ: The Inner Work of Christian Spirituality* (Charlottesville, VA: Hampton Roads Publishing, 2000).

[108] Matthew 6: 33.

[109] James Finley, *The Living Wisdom of Meister Eckhart* (6-CD set of lectures published by SoundsTrue and available at https://www.soundstrue.com/store/meister-eckhart-s-living-wisdom-5959.html

[110] John 10: 30.

[111] John 14: 9.

[112] John 14:20.

[113] Mark 12: 30-31.

[114] John 15: 5.

[115] 1 Corinthians 12: 12-27.

[116] Cynthia Bourgeault, *The Kingdom of Heaven, ibid*.

[117] 1 Corinthians 2:16.

[118] Philippians 2: 5.

[119] The Vulgate was a late fourth century translation of the Bible into Latin done almost single-handedly by St. Jerome. For roughly 1000 years this was *the* Bible of Western Christianity. Most newer translations followed the meaning of the Latin word Jerome used, *poenitentiam*, which refers to regret, repentance, contrition, and a change in mind, missing the more simple and direct meaning of *metanoia* as adopting a higher mind, not simply changing one's mind. This mis-translation of *metanoia* has been described as a "linguistic and theological tragedy" by A.T. Robertson, *"Word Pictures in the New Testament – 2 Corinthians,"* available as a PF from Christian Classics Ethereal Library at www.ccel.org/ccel/robertson_at/wp_2cor.pdf

[120] Matthew 4:17, The Jerusalem Bible.

[121] Edward J. Anton, Repentance: A Cosmic Shift of Mind and Heart (Waltham, MA: Discipleship Publications International, 2005, 31-32).

[122] See Chapter 11, *The Communal Context of Transformation,* in David G. Benner, *Spirituality and the Awakening Self: The Sacred Journey of Transformation* for a much fuller discussion of this communal element of transformation.

[123] See Chapter 1, *Awakening,* in David G. Benner, *Spirituality and the Awakening Self, ibid,* for a discussion of the psychology of Paul's conversion.

[124] Margaret Silf, *Compass Points* (Chicago: Loyola Press, 2009), 224-225.

[125] Sue Woodruff, Meditations with Mechtild of Magdeburg (Santa Fe, NM: Bear & Co., 1982), 46.

[126] Galatians 3:28.

[127] Oliver Sachs, "To See and Not to See," The New Yorker, May 10, 1993, 59.

[128] See, for example, the online documentary, The Overview Effect (https://vimeo.com/55073825), a short film about astronauts' life-changing experiences of seeing Earth from space – a perspective-altering experience often described as the Overview Effect.

[129] Personal conversation between Col. Chris Hadfield and Tom VanGaalen, February 8, 2018.

[130] Acts 9: 1 – 19.

[131] Exodus 3.

[132] Alexis de Tocqueville, Democracy in America (Chicago: University of Chicago Press, 2000, originally published 1835-1840).

[133] It was with this understanding that Alexis de Tocqueville described the foundational values of American culture in 1835, followed 150 years later by Robert Bellah and his colleagues who worked with the same assumptions, updating and extending the analysis. See, Robert N. Bellah, Richard Madsen, William Sullivan, Ann Swidler, Stephen Tipton, Habits of the Heart: Individualism and Commitment in American Life (Berkley, CA: University of California Press, 2007).

[134] Raymond Williams, "Ideas of Nature," in Nature, David Inglis, John Bone, & Rhoda Wilkie (New York, NY: Routledge, 2005), 49.

[135] Sanguin, ibid, 19.

[136] Thomas Berry, The Sacred Universe: Earth, Spirituality and Religion in the Twenty-First Century (New York, NY: Colombia University Press, 2009).

[137] Judy Cannato, *Field of Compassion: How the New Cosmology Is Transforming Spiritual Life* (Notre Dame, IN: Sorin Books: 2010), 16.

[138] The first creation story is found in Genesis 1:1 – 2:3, and the second is found in Genesis 2:4 – 25.

[139] *Thomas Berry: Selected Writings on the Earth Community*, ed. Mary Evelyn Tucker and John Grim (Marynoll, NY: Orbis Books: 2014).

[140] Arne Naess, *Ecology, Community and Lifestyle* (Cambridge, UK: Cambridge University Press, 1989).

[141] Thomas Berry, *The Sacred Universe, ibid*, 78.

[142] Richard Rohr, *Creation as the Body of God*, Daily Meditations, November 9, 2016, https://cac.org/creation-body-god-2016-11-09/

[143] Quoted in Cynthia Bourgeault, *The Wisdom Way of Knowing, ibid*, 52.

[144] Sallie McFague, *The Body of God: An Ecological Theology* (Fortress Press: 1993), xi.

[145] Cynthia Bourgeault, *The Wisdom Way of Knowing: Reclaiming an Ancient Tradition to Awaken the Heart* (Jossey-Bass: 2003), 53.

[146] Thomas Berry, *The Great Work: Our Way into the Future* (Three Rivers Press: 1999), xi.

[147] Sanguin, *ibid,* 157-158.

[148] David G. Benner, *Money Madness and Financial Freedom: The Psychology of Money Meanings and Management* (Calgary, AB: Detselig, 1999). This book is now out of print although it can still sometimes be found in used book stores and online outlets.

[149] Matthew 6: 24.

[150] Alex Eror, *How Consumerism is Used to Control Society*: https://www.highsnobiety.com/2016/11/29/consumerism-social-control/

[151] Victor Lebow, "The Nature of Postwar Retail Competition," *Journal of Marketing* (Spring, Vol. 9, No. 1, 1944), 11-18. The article can be found at http://www.jstor.org/stable/1245520?seq=1#page_scan_tab_contents

[152] See, for example, Annie Leonard, *The Story of Stuff: The Impact of Overconsumption on the Planet, our Communities, and our Health – and How We Can Make it Better* (New York, NY: Free Press, 2011), a highly readable and excellent introduction to the big picture of excessive consumption.

[153] Global Footprint Network. National Footprint Accounts, 2017 Edition. For more information, contact Global Footprint Network at data@footprintnetwork.org

[154] http://data.footprintnetwork.org/#/countryTrends?cn=5001&type=BCpc,EFCpc

[155] Paul Hawken, Amory Lovins and L. Hunter Lovins, *Natural Capitalism* (New York: NY: Little Brown and Company, 1999), 4.

[156] The World Counts: http://www.theworldcounts.com/counters/shocking_environmental_facts_and_statistics/resources_extracted_from_earth#top-facts

[157] *Ibid.*

[158] Cited on *The Global Education Project* webpage, available at: www.theglobaleducationproject.org/earth/food-from-the-oceans.php.

[159] Cited in the 2016 report of Amazon Watch, *From Well to Wheel: The Social, Environmental, and Climate Costs of Amazon Crude*, available at: https://amazonwatch.org/assets/files/2016-amazon-crude-report.pdf

[160] Cited in *Welcome to my jungle … before it's gone* by Karen de Seve, available at: https://www.thefreelibrary.com/Welcome+to+my+jungle+...+before+it%27s+gone.+(Rainforests).-a084307435

[161] Quoted in, Alan During, *How Much is Enough?*, ibid.

[162] Slade, G., *Made to Break: Technology and Obsolescence in America* (Boston, MA: Harvard University Press, 2006). See also, Vance Packard, *The Waste Makers* (New York, NY: Ig Publishing, 2011).

[163] https://inhabitat.com/ecouterre/vanessa-friedman-driving-force-of-fashion-is-planned-obsolescence/

[164] Data drawn from https://blogs.oracle.com/utilities/iphone-6-charging-47-cents, and, https://www.theatlantic.com/technology/archive/2014/10/the-energy-in-things/381557/

[165] Special report of The Atlantic Magazine, *The Energy in Things*: https://www.theatlantic.com/technology/archive/2014/10/the-energy-in-things/381557/

[166] Khadija Farhana, *Ready-made garments in Bangladesh: No longer a forgotten sector*: http://oecdobserver.org/news/fullstory.php/aid/4368/Ready-made_garments_in_Bangladesh:_No_longer_a_forgotten_sector.html

[167] Ashley Westerman, *4 Years After Rana Plaza Tragedy, What's Changed For Bangladeshi Garment Workers?*: https://www.npr.org/sections/parallels/2017/04/30/525858799/4-years-after-rana-plaza-tragedy-whats-changed-for-bangladeshi-garment-workers

[168] See for example, *Twelve Principles of Green Chemistry*, available at https://www.acs.org/content/acs/en/greenchemistry/what-is-green-chemistry/principles/12-principles-of-green-chemistry.html

[169] See the website of Zero Waste International Alliance for more: http://www.zwia.org/standards.html

[170] See the *United Nations World Energy Assessment: Energy and the Challenge of Sustainability*, available at: https://www.undp.org/content/undp/en/home/librarypage/environment-

energy/sustainable_energy/world_energy_assessmentenergyandthechall
engeofsustainability.html

171 https://www.bustle.com/articles/125641-is-recycling-worth-it-the-
answer-might-surprise-you

172 https://www.scientificamerican.com/article/is-recycling-worth-it/

173 John Young and Aaron Sachs, *The Next Efficiency Revolution:
Creating a Sustainable Materials Economy* (Washington, DC:
Worldwatch Institute, 1994), 13.

174 https://www.forbes.com/sites/nealegodfrey/2015/11/01/millennials-
show-boomers-the-benefits-of-barter-pass-it-on/#1e0f251d30cf

175 Comment made by Annie Leonard in her video, *The Story of Stuff*:
https://www.youtube.com/watch?v=9GorqroiqqM

176 Proverbs 30: 8.

177 Luke 3: 11.

178 Matthew 6:24.

179 Matthew 19: 16-30.

180 Matthew 10:37.

181 Cynthia Bourgeault, *The Wisdom Way of Knowing: Reclaiming an
Ancient Tradition to Awaken the Heart* (Hoboken, NJ: Jossey Bass,
2003), 51-53.

182 Luke 6: 45; Matthew 12: 34.

183 Richard Rohr, *Inner Light*: www.cac.org/inner-light-2018-03-23/

184 Mark 12: 30-31.

185 Mark 1: 41-42.

186 Luke 7: 11-16.

187 Matthew 20: 29-34.

188 Matthew 14: 15-21, Matthew 15: 29-39.

189 Matthew 14: 14.

190 Luke 10: 25-37.

[191] Matthew 7: 12.

[192] Mark 12: 28-34.

[193] Mother Teresa, *In the Heart of the World: Thoughts, Stories and Prayers* (Novato, CA: New World Library, 1977), 33.

[194] Matthew 25:40.

[195] Deuteronomy 15:1-18, Proverbs 31: 8-9.

[196] Psalms 72: 12-15, Psalm 103: 6-7.

[197] Casey Lewis, *A Christian View of Social Justice*: https://christianitymatters.com/2016/10/10/a-christian-view-of-social-justice/

[198] 1 Corinthians 12: 1-27.

[199] *Ibid*.

[200] John 15: 5.

Made in the USA
Monee, IL
16 January 2021

57814848R00134